Miniature
Projects for Electronic
Hobbyists

Miniature Projects for Electronic Hobbyists

By Ken W. Sessions, Jr.

TAB BOOKS
Blue Ridge Summit, Pa. 17214

FIRST EDITION

FIRST PRINTING — OCTOBER 1973
SECOND EDITION — OCTOBER 1974

Hardbound Edition: International Standard Book No. 0-8306-3667-6

Paperbound Edition: International Standard Book No. 0-8306-2667-0

Library of Congress Card Number: 73-86762

PREFACE

A project book can probably be considered a fair bargain even if it contains only one circuit of use to the reader, but there is an undeniable waste if the buyer can't get interested in at least several of the published projects. However, building multiple electronic projects, regardless of their overall simplicity, can be an expensive proposition, so it is the rare experimenter who buys a book of projects and undertakes to build every circuit that strikes his fancy—even an **overflowing** junkbox will not be able to supply all parts for **all** projects.

In consideration of these factors, this book has been prepared to encourage a wide range of experimentation with a minimum of parts requirements. Wherever possible, the sections are arranged so that each one describes a basic electronic circuit, with subsectional descriptions on variations of these basics. For example, the section on "The Unijunction Oscillator" includes circuits for a variable audio generator, a metronome for music instruction and timing applications, a code practice oscillator, a signal injector, an rf signal generator, and a tone-burst oscillator for amateur radio and two-way communications use. The individual circuits don't vary much from the basic theme, so parts cost for building every single one of the described projects in this chapter is not substantial.

And so it goes. The result, of course, is to allow you to experiment as much as you like without making an unforgettable gash in your wallet—which makes the book itself a bigger bargain than it would be if it simply listed a large number of simple electronic projects.

But there's more, too. The circuits in this book have one basic characteristic in common: miniaturization. All of them can be built into a container such as a 1 ½ x 4 x 5-inch plastic parts box. All of them use a 9V transistor radio battery for power, which is a good deal safer for beginners than projects designed to operate from 115V household power.

For some reason, the concept of building electronic circuit projects into plastic boxes has been overlooked. Yet the workability of plastic and the ease with which it can be adapted to various applications tend to make the idea particularly attractive from the experimenter's viewpoint. Another important consideration is the low cost of the plastic boxes. If one is ruined for one reason or another, there is no catastrophe. Simply get another of the low-cost "chassis" and start all over.

As you go through this book, you are sure to see applications for circuits beyond those described in the text. Let your imagination govern; go ahead and experiment. If your own idea doesn't work out, at least you'll know you can use the parts for the project on the next page.

The educational value in building the projects in this book is beyond question. Whether you're 13 or over 30, a student or an engineer, you'll enjoy working with these useful circuits. And you'll be happy to note that a large complement of tools is not essential to do a good construction job.

For tools, you'll only need long-nose pliers, wirecutters, a good low-wattage soldering iron (no guns, please—they're nonprofessional and they won't turn out anywhere near as nice a job), rosin core solder, and a very small screwdriver. Items that are handy include a small reamer or hand drill for enlarging the small holes in the phenolic, pliers, and a few various size screwdrivers. You'll need no chassis punches, hacksaws, or other metalworking tools normally associated with electronic construction.

I won't guarantee that every project you build will work right the first time, every time, but I will promise you a very satisfying and rewarding experience with every project you tackle. And I'd be willing to bet you're going to have as much fun building as you will have using what you build.

Ken W. Sessions, Jr.

CONTENTS

Section 4
Practicing With Principles   132

Transformers—Relays—Other Passive Devices—Semiconductor Devices

Index   167

Playing by the Rules

Building things that work is so much fun that it's almost like a game. But, just as with games, in order for you to have fun you have to play according to the rules. Fortunately, there aren't many—but they do exist and they are important. We'll try to cover them sufficiently in this section so they won't need to be referenced again except in emphasis.

Many overzealous newcomers to electronics buy kits and get so anxious to start building that they overlook the little pointers most kit manufacturers publish as preliminary textual data. The result is a job that doesn't look attractive and impressive, or even worse, a job that has no function—for unless the rules are followed at least to a fair degree, the electronic assembly won't work at all. And what good are a lot of electronic parts if they don't perform some unified purpose?

To be sure, some of the rules are written so the finished assembly will **look** attractive, but an attractive-looking assembly is an orderly assembly—and an orderly assembly is one that is easy to troubleshoot by pure observation. What happens when you finish your project, connect the battery, and turn on the power switch, only to find that nothing happens? If you've done a neat wiring job, usually the problem can be solved by carefully examining the assembly and comparing it with the schematic diagram. But if your leads are excessively long, your solder joints lumpy and large, lead routings unconservative, then locating the trouble can be a real headache. More often than not it is easier to start all over than try to troubleshoot a badly wired job. Experience will show you that a little extra time in layout and planning will save you a lot of time in the long run, because even if your unit doesn't work the first time through, you will be able to spot the trouble and fix it without undue effort.

To help you in your initial construction efforts, this chapter lists all the routine construction tips that you should remember as you build. And as you work on your circuits, you can refer to this section from time to time to be certain you haven't overlooked any of the pointers. I hasten to add that most of the material covered in this chapter is already second nature to experimenters who build circuits frequently. Most have learned these pointers the hard way, but if you take the time to read them first and remember what you read, you'll bypass all that "hard luck" schooling.

SOLDERING

The cardinal rule of soldering, when it comes to electronics, concerns nothing other than the type of solder to be used: **Never use anthing other than rosin-core solder.** Rosin-core solder may be called by other names, but always the core will contain at least one grade of rosin. If you have ever used acid-core solder, you know that acid corrodes. If you want a circuit that reacts unpredictably, that corrodes as severely as a bargain battery, then use acid core. But that's the biggest **no-no** there is in electronics hobbying. And if you do use acid-core solder, for pete's sake don't tell anyone about it if you don't want to get laughed out of the experimenters' fraternity.

Rosin-core solder comes in a variety of diameters, and each is good for its own range of functions. For people who use soldering guns rather than irons, diameters up to an eighth of an inch are all right. But only the impetuous would try to use that large a diameter for miniature work. The circuits in this book are built on thin phenolic boards and the overall construction philosophy is very much the same as that employed in printed-circuit construction. As a matter of fact, the finished work will be practically identical in appearance with printed circuitry—at least from the component side of the board. So it will pay to use as thin a solder as possible. I prefer the 60-40 material myself, which is about a thirty-second of an inch in diameter. (The 60-40 is 60 percent lead and 40 percent tin, and has a fairly low melting point.)

Thin solder is easier to handle than thick, and it makes a neater job. For a given solder formula, the thin material melts faster than thick, and it flows freely before the joint you're soldering gets the chance to overheat.

Semiconductors

There are special considerations to bear in mind when you're soldering semiconductors into a circuit. The principal factor to remember is that semiconductors—including silicon diodes, bipolar transistors, unijunctions, FETs, and all the other devices used for the circuits in this book—can tolerate only a limited amount of heat. If that limit is exceeded, the semiconductor will be destroyed.

Until fairly recently, most semiconductors could withstand a junction temperature of not more than 120 degrees Fahrenheit, but rapid improvements in fabrication technology have upped the temperature maximum to well beyond 150 degrees for most silicon devices. Nonetheless, you'd probably be surprised to learn how frequently people who build kits destroy transistors by applying a soldering iron to one of the leads for too long a time. Experienced hobbyists have learned the tricks of minimizing the risks, though. This solder, of course, is one of the tricks, because it melts before the transistor has a chance to get too hot. And a low-wattage iron helps, too, because it doesn't develop enough heat to wipe out a semiconductor unless the heat is applied for an appreciable period. But even more important than either of these techniques is the practice of makeshift "heatsinking."

Heatsinking

Heat has some peculiar characteristics that are worth remembering. The most important, at least with respect to hobbying, is the tendency of heat to "search" for a dissipation route.

Heat is like a disease in a sense; it wants to spread to every area within reach. If you hold the end of a silver knife over the kitchen stove, you'll learn very quickly and very effectively about the rapidity and efficiency with which heat dissipates, because before you have a chance to do much thinking about anything, the heat will spread to the handle and you'll drop the knife. However, if you provide an alternate

11

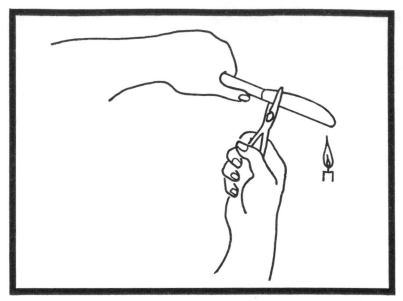

Fig. 1-1. A silver knife held over an open flame will get too hot to handle very quickly. But a pair of pliers, gripping the knife securely between your hand and the flame, will dissipate the heat efficiently and you'll find you can hold the knife for quite a long time before the heat gets excessive.

path for the heat to flow, you'll be able to hang onto the knife for a very long time with no ill effects.

With the knife over the stove, you can provide the additional path by gripping the knife with a pair of pliers somewhere between the flame and your fingers, as shown in Fig. 1-1. The heat travels up the knife blade to the junction of the pliers, then tries to heat both the pliers and the knife. The metal mass of the pliers allows much of the heat to be dissipated into the air about as fast as it can be generated, so the extreme end of the knife will stay as cool as the pliers, at least for a limited amount of time.

The same concept is applied when soldering transistors. Each time you solder a transistor (or diode) lead to a joint, all you have to do is grip the lead securely with your long-nose pliers so that the jaws bite the lead somewhere between the heat and the body of the device. As soon as the joint cools a bit, you can remove the pliers. And then you know there is no chance that any malfunction will be attributable to overheating during the construction process.

Capacitors and Resistors

While most of the heat problems will be nonexistent if you stay with narrow-diameter solder and a low-heat iron, there are a few basics that are good to know when working with passive components such as capacitors and resistors. Both of these device types typically have fairly wide tolerance values in the first place, and if the actual measured value of either happens to be the value imprinted on the body of the device itself, the event can be considered little more than pure coincidence, unless you happen to be a purist and purchase only close-tolerance devices in the first place.

The gist of all this is that the values are liable to be borderline in the first place, and anything you do that might change the value drastically would only be detrimental to the circuit in the end. Heat excesses serve to alter the values of passive components considerably. In some cases, the alteration would simply make the unit closer to its marked value, but if the tolerance is off on the wrong end, it is easy to see that an alteration (as from overheating) would put the value outside the usable limits. So it behooves the builder to use at least some precautions as he builds to minimize the likelihood of value alteration.

Normally, such techniques as plier-gripping of the leads is unnecessary; it is usually sufficient to apply the heat for a short time while the joint makes the solder flow freely, then remove the heat source. But it never hurts to know the effects of overdoing what you do.

The Soldering Iron

Sometimes builders will buy the very best (or at least the most expensive) soldering apparatus, and then complain that it doesn't melt solder properly or that the iron doesn't seem to get hot enough, or that solder "boils" on the surface of the iron without flowing onto the joint to be soldered in the first place. Almost without exception, such faults are attributable to improper care of the iron.

A brand new soldering iron normally has to be conditioned before use. Some irons come preconditioned, though, and need little preliminary care. Irons that are obviously copper at the tip must be heated, coated with solder, allowed to cool, heated again, and recoated before they can be used. Preconditioned irons have a plating that makes such "tinning" unnecessary.

The plated tips are the easiest to use, because they seem to last longer than the pure copper tips and they don't need to be wiped down so frequently. But they are more expensive and not as frequently available in run-of-the-mill electronics houses.

If you have a new iron with an all-copper tip, plug it in and get the tip just hot enough to melt the solder. Apply the solder copiously to the tip and allow it to flow freely over the entire surface. When the surface of the tip has been well coated, unplug the iron but continue to apply solder wastefully. Shake the tip to free it of loose molten solder and keep applying fresh solder from your roll as long as the tip will melt it. Make sure there are no spots anywhere on the tip that haven't taken solder.

When the tip has cooled completely, plug it in again and let it heat for ten minutes without applying new solder. After the ten-minute period, wipe the tip gently with a damp cloth and reapply solder over the entire tip surface. Now you're ready to use the iron.

As you work, keep a damp cloth handy. Every so often, you will notice that the tip will get black; when this happens, the iron will have difficulty in transferring heat to the joint and you'll have to wipe the tip to restore its shininess.

The Art of Soldering

Good soldering is more an art than a science. If the tip of the iron isn't in the condition it should be, you'll have to heat the work excessively before it will take solder successfully. Also, the tip will deteriorate rapidly if it isn't properly groomed during your construction jobs. One way to seriously decrease the life of a soldering tip is to apply solder directly to the tip rather than to the joint being soldered. If you get in the habit of applying solder to the tip rather than to the joint, you will very soon see a dent forming in the tip where you have repeatedly administered the solder. The dent will turn into a hole and before you know if you will have to discard the tip and buy another.

The professional electronic technician learns early that most effective soldering can be accomplished if a shiny soldering tip is applied to the joint for as long as it takes to transfer heat to the joint, then the solder is applied directly to the joint and not to the iron tip. This process is not only the speediest but the best, because it results in a long life for iron tips, a minimum of time for heating the joint, and efficient melting of the solder over the joint.

For miniature work, such as the projects included in this book, it is important to use a fairly fine solder tip. If you want to keep your components close to one another (so that the overall size of the finished circuit can be kept small), you'll have to work in some fairly tight places. A typical example is the soldering of a semiconductor lead to a terminal pin, where the lead has to be very short. The tip of the iron must be applied under the semiconductor device, and in such a way as to allow heat to be applied to the one lead only of the semiconductor and not any of the others that might be situated but a fraction of an inch away.

If you have a fine wedge-shaped soldering tip that is about an eighth of an inch in width, you'll get the hang of close-in soldering in short order; but if you're trying to do the job with a tip that is up to a quarter-inch or more in width, you'll doubtless give it all up in despair—or settle for a job that isn't as neat as you'd like—because wherever the tip touches there will be solder. And if the solder flows where you don't want it to, you'll spend more time trying to desolder than you will soldering.

COMPONENT MOUNTING

Although you won't be using printed circuits, you will be adopting the printed-circuit type of construction for your projects, so it will behoove you to be fairly selective in your component shopping. You'll want to buy the smallest components possible that will fill the bill for a particular project. If you haven't done much electronic construction in the past, you'll probably be surprised to learn that any given component can be obtained in a rather astonishing variety of sizes.

The size variation of components is no doubt attributable to the advances in fabrication technology over the past few years. Five years ago a 10 uF electrolytic capacitor designed for a low voltage (9-16V or so) circuit was more than twice the size of the same unit today. If you buy your parts surplus, you'll no doubt find that they work perfectly satisfactorily, but what you gained in purchase price you lost in miniaturization capability, for the surplus components are almost certain to be of some previous year's vintage. If miniaturization isn't all that important to you, however, go ahead and buy your components from the surplus houses. They'll be a lot cheaper, and should go a long way toward making the size-versus-cost tradeoff acceptable for you. However, if you're going to employ the "plastic-box" concept of chassis mounting that we use in the book, you'll not be able to get by with surplus components.

Another suggestion that bears remembering is to use PC-mount components wherever possible rather than "point-to-point-wiring" components. For potentiometers, this means miniature types that plug directly into the prepunched circuit-board holes (rather than the type that mounts through a ⅜-inch chassis hole). For capacitors, it means radial leads rather than axial leads. An electrolytic capacitor with radial leads is constructed so that both leads extend out on one end of the device, as shown in Fig. 1-2. There is nothing wrong with using axial-lead electrolytics, of course, except that they take up considerably more mounting space. (Axial-lead capacitors have one lead protruding from each end, as shown in Fig. 1-2.)

Unless the circuit descriptions specifically call for higher-wattage resistors, half-watt types are perfectly acceptable for all projects. Quarter-watt resistors are all right, too; but you'll find these cost a great deal more than the half-watt types, and the resultant size differences are not so substantial as to warrant the extra expenditure.

As with soldering, there is a certain "art" in component layout and construction. For the most part, you'll do well to adhere to the layout shown, but if you design variations of the circuits pictured and described, you'll no doubt get involved with some original layout and design work of your own.

In general, layout requires little more than common sense. You will not want to place a capacitor on one extreme part of the board, for example, when it connects to a resistor placed at the other end of the board. If you do, you'll end up with a maze of wires that cross over one another in a back-and-forth zigzag that is virtually impossible to troubleshoot.

Most often, the layout of your board will resemble the printed schematic diagram. Components shown at the left of the diagram will appear on the left side of the board. There will be variations, of course, because the problems of drawing schematics are different from the problems of placing components. But if you try to keep components situated so that there is a minimum of wire crossing under the board, you'll end up with a neat and impressive job.

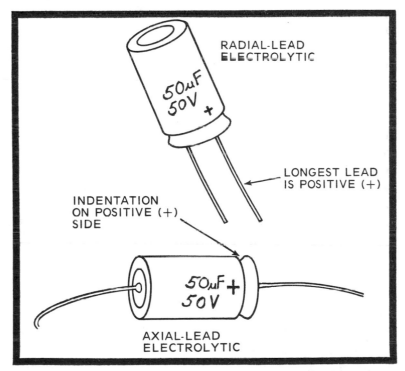

Fig. 1-2. Radial-lead electrolytics are made for printed circuits, and they're ideal for miniature work. Simply plug in the unit so that the leads fit into the board holes. If you use axial-lead electrolytics, pay closer attention to the construction than to the polarity markings; the positive end is always the end with the indentation around the circumference. (Sometimes electrolytics are mismarked.)

Fig. 1-3. G-pattern prepunched phenolic board is ideal for miniature construction projects because the hole layout allows you to simulate the type of job you'd get with a printed circuit. A half-watt resistor (shown here in actual size) spans three holes, and fits neatly into the board if the leads are bent 90 degrees right at the resistor body.

Circuit boards that are "printed" never employ crossed leads, of course, unless both sides of the circuit board involve printed circuitry. If the printed circuit can get by without crossed leads, so can the point-to-point circuit such as you'll be working with. If you do your own layout, you'll find that this aspect of construction can be much like a puzzle—how to route the leads so that no lead ever crosses another. But this takes a lot of time and is of only dubious value in the end. The best bet is to make a try for a minimum of wire crossing and settle for whatever you have to without worrying about it.

The final point to consider is the actual mounting of the components. You will find that most components will plug directly into the prepunched phenolic G-pattern board, which is pictured in actual size in Fig. 1-3. Half-watt resistors are not quite as long as the space consumed by three board holes, so they plug in nicely if the leads are bent at right angles to the device and the bends are right against the resistor bodies. Radial-lead electrolytic capacitors also plug in nicely, except in rare cases. And virtually all trimmer resistors and capacitors fit the same way. You'll find working with the G-pattern board almost as easy as working with a printed circuit, and a whole lot more fun.

When you plug a device into the board so that the leads extend to the other side of the board, make certain you push the leads all the way into the board so that the devices rest against the board as shown in Fig. 1-4. This makes the components all stand straight up or lie perfectly flat, and results in a neater appearing job than one in which the leads are just poked through in a haphazard manner.

Keystone Electronics manufactures push-in terminal pins for G-pattern boards, and you'll find these quite useful when mounting transistors and other devices that won't plug right into the board. They also make handy junctions when a number of wires must be joined at one point. These are expensive, though, so we'll try to restrict their use to an as-necessary basis. For most joints, you can simply wrap the joining leads together on the underside of the board and apply a little solder.

THE PLASTIC-BOX CHASSIS

When your circuit has been put together and it operates the way you want it to, you'll want to enclose it in a chassis of sorts. The plastic boxes that are readily available in most five-and-dime stores are ideal for this. You'll want a size that will hold the board and enclose the complete circuit even when the box is closed. For most applications, the 4 ¼ x 5 ½-inch size is just right, but if your components are not as small as the ones I used in building up the initial projects, you may have to get something a little bigger. You'll never have to get a box

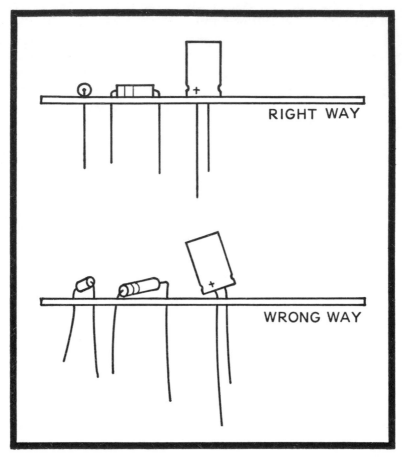

Fig. 1-4. If components are not pushed firmly onto the board surface, the components will end up loosely mounted and the job's appearance will be sloppy. The board itself offers a great deal of stability to mounted components if they are pushed all the way in.

thicker than 1 ½ inches, though, unless your parts are of World War II vintage.

Naturally, having the circuit in a box will be of little use unless you can operate the unit without opening the box. And operating the enclosed circuit from outside the box means incorporating holes in the box surface for mounting controls and the like.

Fortunately, you won't need metalworking tools for working the plastic. Your soldering iron should be the only tool you need, assuming you have some degree of ingenuity, of course. If you have to cut holes in the plastic, simply apply the hot tip of your soldering iron to the box surface and "cut" the area. If you have to drill holes for control shafts or switches, just push the hot soldering tip through the box surface wherever you want the control to be mounted.

Be sure to clean the tip of the iron when you have used it for a saw or drill, though. The plastic will gum up the soldering tip and make it unusable until after you've cleaned it. It can be easily cleaned, though, and the molten plastic will not deleteriously affect it.

READING COMPONENT VALUES

The biggest mystery in electronic construction—at least to the novitiate—is the coding used by manufacturers to mark the values of resistors and capacitors. There are a number of systems by which capacitors are marked, so these will not be mentioned in this book (even experienced constructionists are not familiar with all the systems in use). Resistors, though, are another story. There is but one method of coding resistors, and no experimenter can be really comfortable in his work unless he either knows this code or has a reference for checking the values of resistors he has purchased.

Resistor coding is accomplished with stripes of various colors. If you hold a resistor so that the colored stripes are on the left side of the device body, you can easily determine the value of the resistor. The first stripe tells you the first number in the overall value; the second stripe tells you the second number in the value. The third stripe tells you how many zeroes follow the first two numbers. It's really that simple—almost.

There are a few complications, such as decimal values and tolerances, but the three basic stripes are those of chief concern. The table of Fig. 1-5 shows the numerical values assigned to the various colors.

Remembering the resistor color code isn't too hard if you employ some sort of system. Try to think of a cute saying or a rhyme in which the first letter of each word is the same as the initial letter of each sequential color in the code. It's another matter to remember the verse you make up, however. When I

A

COLOR	1ST DIGIT	2ND DIGIT	MULTIPLIER	TOLERANCE (percent)
Black	0	0	1	
Brown	1	1	10	
Red	2	2	100	
Orange	3	3	1,000	
Yellow	4	4	10,000	
Green	5	5	100,000	
Blue	6	6	1,000,000	
Violet	7	7	10,000,000	
Gray	8	8	100,000,000	
White	9	9	1,000,000,000	
Gold			.1	5
Silver			.01	10
No color				20

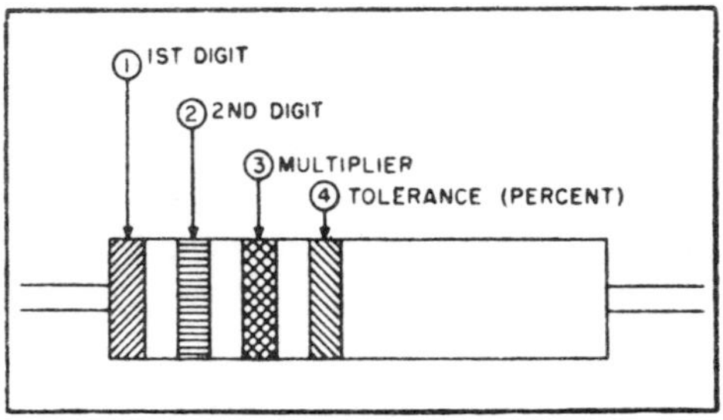

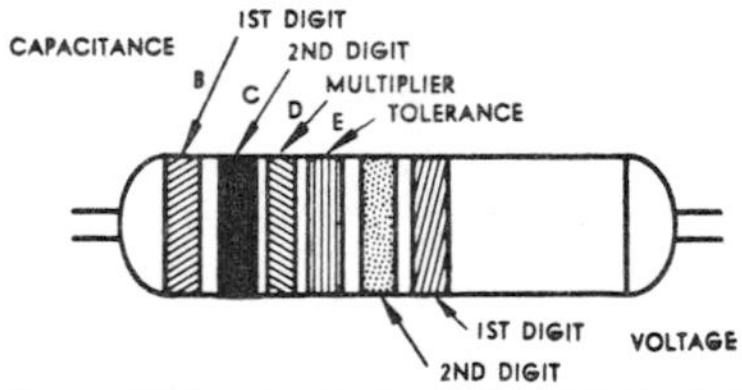

COLOR	CAPACITANCE			TOLERANCE (PERCENT)	VOLTAGE RATING	
	1ST DIGIT	2ND DIGIT	MULTIPLIER		1ST DIGIT	2ND DIGIT
BLACK	0	0	1	±20	0	0
BROWN	1	1	10		1	1
RED	2	2	100		2	2
ORANGE	3	3	1,000	−30	3	3
YELLOW	4	4	10,000	±40	4	4
GREEN	5	5	100,000	± 5	5	5
BLUE	6	6	1,000,000		6	6
VIOLET	7	7			7	7
GRAY	8	8			8	8
WHITE	9	9		±10	9	9

Fig. 1-5. Resistor color code.

was in college, I invented this one: Big Ben Rings Out, "Young Girls Buy Volkswagens, George Washington." But in retrospect, I must say that the colors themselves might be easier to remember than the verse. It isn't too difficult to remember that black is zero. Think of the earth before man came, before there was light. That was nothingness, blackness—consequently, zero. Brown seems the next likely step from black. There's only one other B to remember, which is blue. There are two Gs, however, and the only way I know of to remember which is which is to study the chart for enough time to implant the sequence firmly in your mind.

There are still ways to remember some of the colors, though, if you need such devices. Green is five. You've heard of "green thumbs" and you've heard of people being "all thumbs." So, by association, you think of green by associating it with five green thumbs. The other G is, of course, gray; and it is not nearly so common in resistor markings as the colors from black to violet.

If you haven't had experience with the color code, study the chart for a few minutes and see if you can apply the code to some real cases. Assume you have a resistor whose first three bands are yellow, violet, and red. Remember that the first band gives you the first digit of the value and the second band gives you the second digit. The third band is the multiplier, and tells you not the number itself but the number of zeroes following the first two digits.

The value of the resistor colored yellow, violet, and red, then, is 4700 (ohms). The first band is yellow (4), the second violet (7), and the third red (for 2 zeroes).

Sometimes you'll see another band, either gold or silver. For the projects in this book, the final band is nonessential. If there is no fourth band, the resistor should be within 20 percent of its marked value. If the fourth band is silver, the resistor should be within 10 percent of its marked value; if gold, the tolerance is 5 percent.

Section 2

The Unijunction Oscillator

Although not nearly so esoteric as the name makes it seem, the unijunction transistor is one of the most versatile devices in man's semiconductor arsenal. Its capabilities are so broad that only a few other components need to be used with it to make quite a wide array of diverse circuits. This section describes but a few of the basic variations of a unijunction transistor oscillator. If you like to experiment, you will almost certainly find applications beyond those shown in the circuits of this section. And if you're the daring type, you will be able to see how to apply the unijunction in circuits you design yourself.

The basic unijunction oscillator circuit is pictured in Fig. 2-1. If you're new to electronics, don't let the form scare you. The schematic diagram pictured is simply the engineer's shorthand method of describing the way the circuit components connect to one another. As we go along, you'll be able to read and understand these "shorthand pictures" as well as the most experienced home constructionist.

THE UNIJUNCTION TRANSISTOR

Unlike ordinary transistors, which have two diode-type junctions, the unijunction transistor has but one—even though the device has three leads. Picture the unijunction as a bar of metal with a lead connected to its center, as shown in Fig. 2-2. The bar is usually made of silicon that has been doped with impurities to give it a negative characteristic. The lead protruding from the center of the bar is embedded in a pocket of positive-type material. The operation of the unijunction transistor is based on the ability of an applied voltage to change the resistivity of the bar.

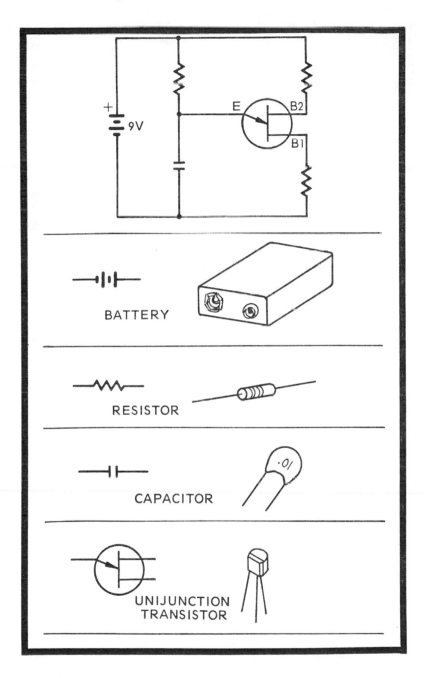

Fig. 2-1. Basic circuit of unijunction oscillator. At right are schematic symbols shown with pictorial representations of each component.

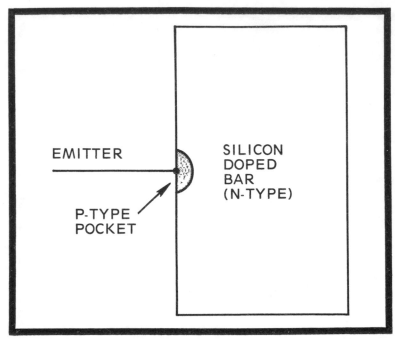

Fig. 2-2. The unijunction is so called because of its one junction where the p-type emitter connects to the n-type bar of silicon. In practice, the bar has a lead connected to each end. The bar leads are called "bases." The upper end is referred to as "base 2" and the lower end as "base 1."

If a battery is connected to the ends of the bar, current will flow across the bar as if it were a wire. The amount of current flow, of course, is determined by the resistivity of the bar—the better it conducts, the greater the current flow. There will be a definite voltage value at the positive-electrode pocket, since the total battery voltage appears across the whole bar.

The positive-negative junction where the emitter lead is embedded in the bar is reverse biased, which means that only a small amount of current flows in the emitter circuit. (A positive-negative junction allows current to flow only one way.) However, if an external voltage is applied to the emitter, an interesting thing happens: As the emitter voltage is increased, there is a point at which the applied emitter voltage equals the voltage at that point in the bar (plus the forward voltage drop of the positive-negative junction). At this point (referred to as the peak point emitter voltage) the emitter junction is reverse biased, and current is caused to flow from the emitter into the silicon bar. When this happens, current flows furiously for a brief period because the bar appears to lose resistivity suddenly. The more current flows, the more it wants to flow, because the very passage of current across the bar tends to lower the resistivity, until the bar actually seems to have a negative resistance.

When the electron flow is more than the bar can handle (at saturation), the resistivity increases sharply again. In practice, the emitter voltage is normally provided by a capacitor. When the capacitor discharges through the emitter, the unijunction will return to its original off state and the process can repeat itself.

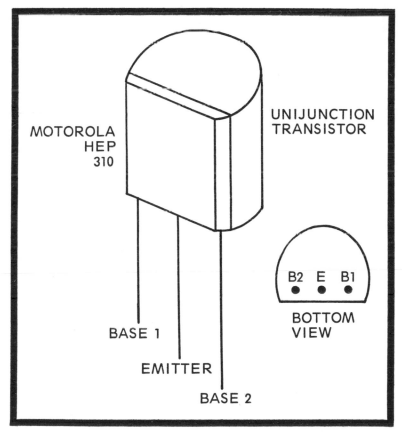

Fig. 2-3. The Motorola HEP 310 unijunction transistor is actually much smaller than it appears here. You could probably hold at least a hundred in your hand.

The time period required for the complete process is amazingly short—so short, in fact, that hundreds of thousands of the cycles can be completed in but one second.

While the above explanation is well simplified and ad-mittedly sketchy, it should serve to show the basic operation of the unijunction transistor. The device itself, shown in the sketch of Fig. 2-3, has three leads: two base leads and the emitter. In the device pictured, the Motorola HEP 55, the center lead is the emitter. Base 2 is the equivalent of the top of the bar pictured in Fig. 2-2; base 1 represents the bottom of the silicon bar.

In the schematic (Fig. 2-1), the unijunction is represented by the large circle with the slanted arrow in it. Resistors are indicated by zigzags. The interconnecting lines are wires. The two parallel lines separating the interconnecting wire denote a capacitor. The plus sign tells us the capacitor is an electrolytic type. See how simple it is to read a schematic diagram once you understand the engineer's symbology. In case you haven't already guessed it, all you have to do to make up the circuit is connect the units as they are shown, using wire to interconnect the components and solder to secure the joints. If you're ready to apply the circuit into a useful project, read on.

Project 1

Code Practice Oscillator

If you're new to electronics experimentation and you think you're going to have fun with it, you might like to "go all the way" and get into one of the "funnest" of the fun aspects of electronics hobbying—amateur radio. Getting an amateur radio license—becoming a ham operator—isn't difficult if you're going for the Novice class license. The FCC will issue you a "ticket" and assign call letters to you if you pass a very simple electronics test and a Morse code sending and receiving test. You'll have no trouble with the theory if you build up a few projects in the book, for the questions on the FCC exam deal mostly with the very basic elements: resistances being measured in ohms, capacitances being measured in farads, and the like. There are a few simple questions with regard to FCC operating rules, of course, but these are easy to learn if you simply send for information about the exam from the FCC or purchase one of TAB's several fine books on the subject.

LEARNING THE MORSE CODE

You must demonstrate an ability to send and receive Morse code at a rate of five words per minute, which is a whole lot easier than it sounds (five words per minute is only one character per second). Easy as it is, though, you won't be able to do it without practice, regardless of how well you study. You simply **must** have a code oscillator to practice on.

We'll get into construction of the code oscillator you can build in a few moments; but first we'll present you with a few facts, such as what the characters are and how best to learn to send and receive. The characters themselves are presented in Fig. 2-4; they consist of the letters A to Z, the numbers 0 through 9, and various punctuation marks.

A	·—	didah
B	—···	dahdididit
C	—·—·	dahdidahdit
D	—··	dahdidit
E	·	dit
F	··—·	dididahdit
G	——·	dahdahdit
H	····	didididit
I	··	didit
J	·———	didahdahdah
K	—·—	dahdidah
L	·—··	didahdidit
M	——	dahdah
N	—·	dahdit
O	———	dahdahdah
P	·——·	didahdahdit
Q	——·—	dahdahdidah
R	·—·	didahdit
S	···	dididit
T	—	dah
U	··—	dididah
V	···—	didididah
W	·——	didahdah
X	—··—	dahdididah
Y	—·——	dahdidahdah
Z	——··	dahdahdidit
1	·————	didahdahdahdah
2	··———	dididahdahdah
3	···——	didididahdah
4	····—	dididididah
5	·····	dididididit
6	—····	dahdidididit
7	——···	dahdahdididit
8	———··	dahdahdahdidit
9	————·	dahdahdahdahdit
0	—————	dahdahdahdahdah
	·—·—·—	didahdidahdidah
	——··——	dahdahdididahdah
?	··——··	dididahdahdidit

Fig. 2-4. The International Morse Code. Note the manner in which the sound of each character is presented. If you think of the characters in the "words" given, you'll have little trouble learning the code.

When you take the code test (it can be administered by any General class amateur radio operator), the examiner will send at the rate of five words per minute, and he will send a variety of characters. The punctuation marks, if he sends them, will count as two characters because they are so much more difficult to learn than the letters (and they take longer to send because there are so many "digits" in each one). The same is true for numbers. You will have five minutes to take the test, and all you have to do to pass is copy any 25 characters in a row without a mistake. (This is the equivalent to a one-minute period of copying at the five-word-per-minute rate.)

To assist you in learning the code, make sure you get in the habit of thinking of each letter or number or punctuation mark as a complete character in itself. They all consist of dots and dashes, of course, but you can't think fast enough if you restrict your thinking to terms of dots and dashes. Each letter has a "sound" all its own.

Code experts teach you to call dashes "dahs" and dots "dits." A Z then would be dah-dah-dit-dit rather than dash-dash-dot-dot. The nice part of the dah-dit technique is that you can increase the speed considerably by saying, rather than dah-dah-dit-dit, "dahdahdidit"—running it all together to get it out quicker. This may seem academic, but the experience of many prospective hams over a large number of years has proved that the speedup process of running the characters together in this manner results in prompt improvement in overall sending and receiving ability.

Another way to improve speed, once the characters are memorized, is to think in dahs and dits as you send. Normally, you won't have the time to do this type of thinking as you receive, because the characters seem to come at you too hot and heavy to do any thinking at all. But by thinking the "dah-dit" terms as you send, you help implant the characters in your mind so they will be remembered when the time comes for you to demonstrate your code-sending and -receiving prowess to the FCC examing appointee.

Another helpful idea, once you have the characters memorized, is to read everything you see in terms of dahs and dits. When you're eating breakfast, read the cereal box. But instead of sending off for the electric trains or kites you're offered, just ignore the meaning of the words and send all the characters mentally. As you go to school or work, read all the signs the same way. Before long, you'll find yourself dreaming the code. And then you're on the way to passing the test. Once the characters start coming to you in your sleep—and they will, make no mistake about that—you've got your subconscious so triggered that with only a modicum of additional effort you can go on and try for the General class amateur license—the one that is the creamiest of them all in terms of operating privileges.

COMPONENT CONSIDERATIONS

The schematic diagram for the code practice oscillator is shown in Fig. 2-5. In addition to the electronic parts, you'll need either a small speaker (60 to 100 ohms) or a pair of headphones (to allow you to hear what you send), and a telegraph key. Chances are you'll be able to find all the parts you need, including the speaker or earphones, at your local electronics supply store. In any event, your dealer will be able to order any part for you that he does not stock. Figure 2-6 is a list of all the parts you need. Bear in mind as you look over the parts list that most of the components will be usable for other projects described in this section, so there won't be much wasted if you give up on your code practice and decide to try something else.

Acquiring The Parts

Only rarely will you be able to go to one store and buy all parts that you need. Unless you want to wait while the store orders parts especially for you, you may have to settle for values other than those shown. When I bought parts, for example, I was unable to obtain the telegraph key or the speaker. Since I happened to have a set of headphones on hand from my early days in ham radio, I opted for the 47-ohm resistor substitute shown in Fig. 2-5B. But that didn't settle the problem of getting a key.

Telegraph keys are actually very simple devices, and I've heard of people making them with bits and scraps from the hardware store. But I didn't want to get involved in any side

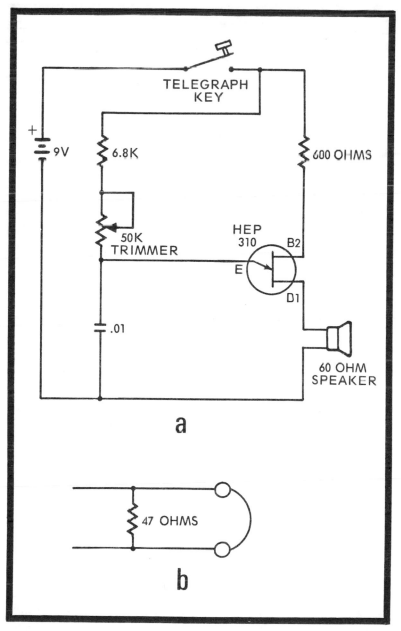

Fig. 2-5. The basic schematic diagram for the code practice oscillator is shown at A. The earphone-and-resistor circuit shown at B can be used in place of the speaker if the right value speaker is unavailable. The best value for the earphones is an impedance of 2000 ohms or so, though lower impedance types will operate satisfactorily.

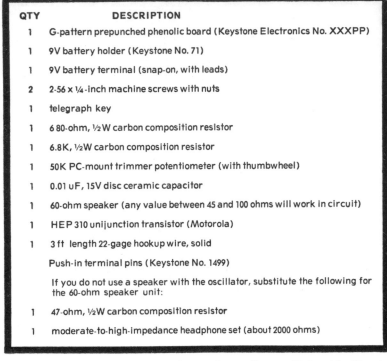

QTY	DESCRIPTION
1	G-pattern prepunched phenolic board (Keystone Electronics No. XXXPP)
1	9V battery holder (Keystone No. 71)
1	9V battery terminal (snap-on, with leads)
2	2-56 x ¼-inch machine screws with nuts
1	telegraph key
1	6 80-ohm, ½W carbon composition resistor
1	6.8K, ½W carbon composition resistor
1	50K PC-mount trimmer potentiometer (with thumbwheel)
1	0.01 uF, 15V disc ceramic capacitor
1	60-ohm speaker (any value between 45 and 100 ohms will work in circuit)
1	HEP 310 unijunction transistor (Motorola)
1	3 ft length 22-gage hookup wire, solid
	Push-in terminal pins (Keystone No. 1499)
	If you do not use a speaker with the oscillator, substitute the following for the 60-ohm speaker unit:
1	47-ohm, ½W carbon composition resistor
1	moderate-to-high-impedance headphone set (about 2000 ohms)

Fig. 2-6. Parts list for the unijunction code practice oscillator. You'll note that more parts are listed here than are shown on the schematic; that's because the schematic doesn't show such passive elements as the circuit board, battery holder, box, etc.

projects, so I bought a simple spring-return switch, officially known as a normally open, momentary-contact, single-pole switch. This switch and all the other parts, except for the speaker or headphones, is shown in Fig. 2-7. Since the parts are not identified in the photo, you may not recognize them. In the upper left corner of the sheet is the momentary-contact switch which serves as my key. Below that are the resistors— the 6800-ohm resistor (blue' gray' red) is at the left, the 680-ohn resistor is directly adjacent (blue, gray, brown), and the 47-ohm resistor (yellow, violet, black) is not shown. Next to the resistors is the Keystone battery holder, the 2-56 x ½-inch nuts and bolts (I had to settle for ⅜-inch bolts because I had those on hand), and the push-in terminal pins. The 50K trimmer potentiometer is shown along with the 0.01 uF disc ceraminc capacitor and the unijunction transistor. Finally, the 2 x 3-inch board with its holes spaced at 100 mil intervals (G pattern) and the battery connector with 6-inch leads are shown.

The Key. If you can't buy a telegraph key (and you really should if you're going to be serious in your code study, for nothing is a good substitute for a good key) you can buy a momentary-contact switch as I did or you can make a simple affair. What you need to make one is a thin metal strip from a tin can and a round knob such as the type you find on small drawers and cupboards.

There are several ways for you to put various pieces together and come up with a keying device. After all, a key is

Fig. 2-7. Parts required for the code practice oscillator. Not shown are the wires, speaker or earphone, or telegraph key. The momentary-contact switch (upper left) replaces the key. The 47-ohm resistor is unnecessary if a 60- to 100-ohm speaker is available.

nothing more than a pair of contacts that close when you want them to.

If you use the tin-can approach, you'll need tin snips and a couple of extra nuts and bolts. Cut the tin as shown in the sketch of Fig. 2-8. The strip should be about ½ inch wide, but be sure to file it to avoid the possibility of getting cut on the edge. Use a hammer and nail to put a small hole in each end of the strip. Secure the knob to one end with a wood screw and tighten it. You can attach the other end of the strip to the plastic box with a nut and a bolt. To do that, you'll have to burn a small hole in the box so the bolt will pass through.

You need one other nut and bolt, which should be mounted through the plastic box directly under the knob. When you push the knob down, you'll want the knob's wood screw to contact the head of the bolt in the plastic box. The electrical connections to the two through-box bolts can be accomplished from under the surface of the box cover.

If you buy a momentary-contact switch, mounting it is simply a matter of melting a hole in the plastic box cover that is large enough in diameter to accommodate the collar bushing of the switch. Again, electrical connections will be made under the surface of the box top.

The Resistors. The resistor values shown are very common, so you'll probably have no trouble getting them. However, in the event your supplier is out of them, bear in mind that you have a lot of leeway here, for resistor tolerances in this circuit are not critical.

In electronics, the letter K stands for thousand, so you will find 1000-ohm resistors referred to frequently as 1K resistors. The 6800-ohm resistor might be stocked in the store as a 6.8K unit.

If you can't buy a 6.8K, the next standard low-cost value is 4.7K, which will operate perfectly satisfactorily. The only effect you will notice when using the lower value will be a different basic pitch of the oscillator. Since you will have a variable control (the trimmer) with which to change the pitch anyway, don't worry about having to settle for some value other than 6.8K.

You shouldn't stray too far from the values shown for the other two resistors. A 470-ohm value is all right in place of the 680-ohm device, but if the tolerance of the 470-ohm resistor is off on the low side, the unit might not work properly. If your supplier can't give you the 680-ohm resistor, he might be able to measure a few of his 470-ohm units in order to give you one that is either right on its marked value or slightly over.

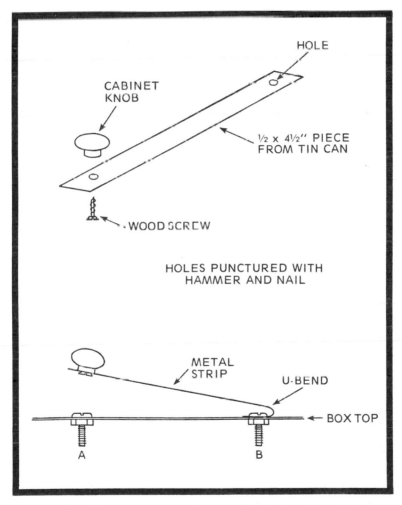

Fig. 2-8. You can make your own key by affixing a knob to a thin metal strip as shown. Connect the assembly to the box top as shown so that when the knob is pressed down, the wood screw touches the through-box bolt at A. The two electrical tie points are A and B.

The 47-ohm resistor can be a little higher in value than that shown, but the audio volume will be degraded substantially if you try to get by with a lower resistance value. The next standard size up is 51 ohms, which will be ideal. The trouble with buying a 51-ohm resistor is that it will have a tolerance of 5 percent, which will probably cost you about twice as much as a 47-ohm resistor.

You can also "make" your own resistor by placing several other values of resistance in series or parallel combinations to get the value you want. When you string resistors in a series arrangement, simply add the values of each to arrive at the total resistance value for the string. If you place two like values in parallel, the total resisance is halved. In Fig. 2-9, two parallel 100-ohm resistors are connected to make a resistor whose value is 50 ohms. In Fig. 2-10, a 470-ohm, a 150-ohm, and a 47-ohm resistor are connected in series to make a resistor that has a resistance of 667 ohms from end to end:

Parallel resistances aren't always halved, by the way. The total resistance value is always less than the lowest value used. But this book is not for teaching math, so we'll steer clear of this aspect of value calculating.

The Capacitor. Disc ceramic capacitors are sold according to value in microfarads (and sometimes picofarads) and also according to the voltage of the circuit in which they will be used. Since the capacitor used in this circuit will see voltages that never exceed 9V, the voltage you will ask for will be 15, which is the nearest standard voltage value above your working potential of 9V.

Like resistors, capacitors can be "fabricated" from existing types. But the method for doing it is exactly the opposite from resistors. You parallel capacitors to get a total value that is the sum of all the capacitors in parallel, and you string them in series if you want a value less than any of the units you have on hand. A pair of 0.005 uF disc ceramic capacitors in parallel results in a capacitor whose total value is 0.01 uF. A pair of 0.02 uF capacitors in series will yield a capacitor whose end-to-end value is 0.01 uF.

The Trimmer Potentiometer. It is unlikely that you'll find a trimmer potentiometer exactly like the one pictured in Fig. 2-7. These little devices come in a huge assortment of configurations, and it matters little which type you use. If possible, try to get one made for printed-circuit mounting, because the three leads will plug directly into the G-pattern board. Try to avoid a full-size potentiometer, though, because you'll have more trouble mounting it than the code practice oscillator is worth.

If you're building the unit from junkbox parts, and just happen to have a standard panel-mount potentiometer lying around, go ahead and use it, but you'll have to mount it through the cover of the box because it will be too big to fit inside the box with the lid closed. You can use a control with either a **linear** or an **audio** taper. An audio-taper potentiometer

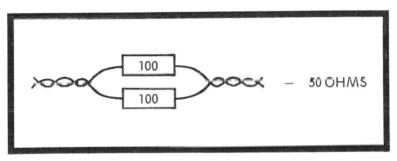

Fig. 2-9. If you parallel like values, the resultant value is equal to the value of one resistor divided by the number of resistors in the group.

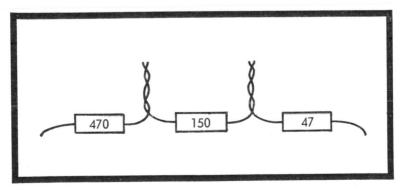

Fig. 2-10. Series resistors yeild a value equal to the sum of the resistances.

does not allow even tuning across the potentiometer's entire range. At the halfway point of the control, as a matter of fact, one side of the wiper arm will have only 10 percent of the control's total resistance and the other side will have 90 percent of it. With a linear-taper potentiometer, however, at the halfway setting, the resistance is divided evenly over the control's range so that the resistance on each side of the wiper arm will be exactly the same.

Some trimmer; can be adjusted only with a screwdriver. I find it more convenient to buy only trimmers that have "thumbwheels" so that the potentiometer can be adjusted with the fingertips.

When you buy the trimmer, the store's counter man will probably ask you whether you want a vertical or a horizontal mounting type. It doesn't make any difference from an operational viewpoint. I personally like the horizontal mounting devices because they have a little more mechanical stability than the vertical types. But this is only a matter of personal preference.

CONSTRUCTION PREPARATIONS

When you have all the parts together, and all the tools you'll require, it will be time for you to get started with the construction. But if you've never built a kit or electronic projects before, you'll probably be tempted to work at such an unlikely spot as the kitchen table. Don't do it; not only will you be likely to generate ill will among other members of your family (who just might want to eat while you're working on your code practice oscillator), but you'll risk scarring the tabletop with molten solder or scratching it with wire ends. Your best bet is to set up a small table or bench in a remote area of the house, away from the hustle and bustle of the family's day-to-day activities. This will allow you to leave your project before it's finished if necessary, and return to it with nothing disturbed during your absence.

Allow yourself plenty of room, too. You need a household electrical outlet somewhere nearby where you can plug in your soldering iron, but try to arrange your work area so the wall plug is on your right (assuming you're right-handed, that is). If you have a wall plug in front of you on the left and you're right-handed, you will be under constant irritation from the soldering iron's cord getting in the way of your work.

If you're tackling a big project, such as one of the many fine kits produced by the Heath Company, you'll want to arrange all your parts in a container of some sort, such as an empty egg carton. For such simple projects as the unijunction oscillator, however, where the parts complement is relatively small, this won't be necessary. Place all your parts on one side of the work area, and put the tools on the other side. Get the iron heated up and conditioned as described in Section I, and you're ready to go.

BUILDING THE UNIT

The first thing to do is determine the layout of the parts. The best way to do this is to plug all the parts into the board in the way they'll be situated when the job is completed—as sort of a "dry run." Once you do this, you can mentally interconnect all the wires to be sure that all the components are rationally laid out and there are no unduly long leads traversing the board. Once you establish a basic layout for all the parts, you should sketch the layout on a piece of scratch paper to help you remember where you've decided to place each component. You can rely on your memory, but if your memory is anything like mine, it will fail you when you need it the most.

Component Mounting

The first step is to install the battery holder on the board. The holes will line up fairly well with the mounting holes of the battery holder, but the bolts will be a little too large in diameter to go through the board, so you'll have to ream them or drill them with a little hand drill. Place the battery holder in position on the board and mark through the battery holder's mounting holes with a sharp pencil.

If you don't have a hand drill or reamer, you can use the blade of a small screwdriver to enlarge the board holes enough to accept the 2-56 bolts. But be careful and don't try to work too fast. The first time I tried that technique, the screwdriver slipped and I incurred a superficial wound—not serious, but enough to make me think twice about using a screwdriver for reaming.

Mount the battery holder to the board using the 2-56 bolts and nuts. Be sure the bolts go down through the board and holder from the top, or the battery won't fit into the holder.

After the battery holder is mounted, insert the seven push-in terminals. Three of the terminals should be mounted in a close group so that the unijunction transistor can be plugged into them and soldered in place. Figure 2-11 is a sketch that shows the layout I used. The terminal-pin positions are indicated by the elongated C shapes on the sketch.

Once the terminals have been inserted (they don't go into the board easily, by the way—you'll have to gently urge them in with your long-nose pliers), you can mount the resistors and capacitor. Don't mount the trimmer yet, though, because it doesn't stay in its position without being soldered there. Bend the resistor leads at a right angle where the leads enter the resistor body. You'll find the resistors will plug right into the board. The components can be temporarily secured to the board surface by bending the leads under the board. Once you get all the components in position (except for the trimmer, of course), you can begin the interconnection under the board. But don't solder until all the parts have been connected together in the way they'll be when the job is completed. This concept allows you to correct any wiring errors you might make without getting involved with the problems of desoldering, which can be a headache even for the most experienced hobbyist.

Wiring

The wiring is about the easiest part. Bring one of the leads from the 680-ohm resistor to the underside of the pin where the B2 lead of the unijunction transistor will plug in. The other end of that resistor will tie to the push-in terminal on the right.

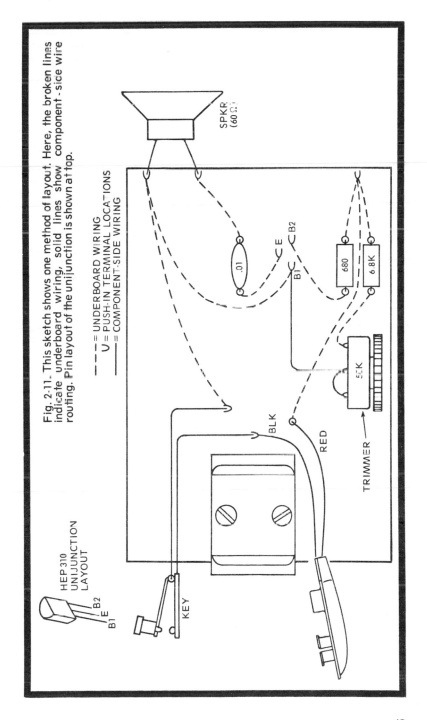

Fig. 2-11. This sketch shows one method of layout. Here, the broken lines indicate underboard wiring, solid lines show component-side wire routing. Pin layout of the unijunction is shown at top.

- - - - = UNDERBOARD WIRING
V = PUSH-IN TERMINAL LOCATIONS
—— = COMPONENT-SIDE WIRING

SPKR
(60 Ω)

.01

E
B2
B1

680

6.8K

ECK

TRIMMER

BLK

RED

KEY

HEP 310
UNIJUNCTION
LAYOUT

B2
E
B1

43

You won't be able to do much other wiring unless you plug the trimmer potentiometer into the board. If the pin of the trimmer protrudes far enough through the board, it will simplify the wiring for you. You can look at the sketch to see how the disc capacitor interconnects. Wrap one of the disc capacitor's leads around the appropriate push-in terminal and cut off the excess lead with your wirecutters, saving the cut-off lead for use with the trimmer. Tie the other end of the capacitor to the nearest trimmer pin and trim off the excess from this lead, too. Use the saved piece to tie the other two trimmer pins together. If you wrap the trimmer pins firmly with the leads, you won't have to do any soldering to hold the trimmer to the chassis.

Connect the 6.8K resistor between the upper trimmer pin and the proper push-in terminal, wrapping the leads securely at each tie point. If you have a fairly long lead left, you can run it from the pin of the trimmer where the capacitor connects to the emitter lead of the unijunction (if you've used the HEP 310 device recommended, the emitter lead will be the center one of the three-pin group).

Double-check all your wiring now to make certain you haven't made any mistakes. Check the wiring first against the sketch of my unit (Fig. 2-11). If you used some other layout than mine, follow your connections as you look at the schematic diagram. Once you are absolutely certain that all your components are installed in the proper positions and that all wires are correctly interconnected, it is all right to start soldering. You will note we haven't yet connected the battery connector, the speaker or earphones, or the key. These will be the final steps.

Solder carefully, making sure you don't put too much solder on any joint—but be careful to get the joint hot enough to make solder flow freely over it. As soon as a joint is secured with solder, you can cut off all the excess wire from it so that it makes a nice, neat joint under the board.

After soldering, insert the transistor into position so the three leads plug into the three push-in terminals you have grouped for this purpose. It might be a good idea to bend the leads of the unijunction with your long-nose pliers to allow it to plug into the pins easily. Once the unijunction is in the circuit, you can solder the leads to the pins. Use extreme caution here, though, to avoid overheating the semiconductor. Don't use any more heat than is necessary to make the solder flow over the pin and the lead inserted there. As soon as the solder flows well, remove the soldering tip and allow the lead to cool. When it has cooled enough for you to touch it, connect the next lead the same way.

Push the leads from the battery connector into the board at some convenient place and tie a knot in the leads under the board to act as a strain relief. Then solder the red lead to the push-in terminal where the 6.8K resistor is attached and solder the black lead to the lower push-in terminal where the 0.01 uF capacitor is connected. If you have done all your wiring properly, the only items left to install are the speaker (or earphone-resistor combination) and the key. Since push-in terminal pins have been provided for this purpose, there should be no complications.

Checkout

Connect the speaker terminals to the points shown in the schematic diagram (or simply refer to the sketch) with a pair of wires, and do the same with the key or switch. If you haven't made any mistakes, you're ready to go. Press the key and the speaker or phone should reproduce a nice clean tone. To change the tone's pitch, simply adjust the trimmer.

If the code practice oscillator doesn't work the first time, you'll get your chance to try a little troubleshooting. The first thing you must do is painstakingly check out all your wiring. No matter how many times you've traced the circuit through before, start from scratch and repeat the entire procedure. Be especially watchful for wires that are touching but shouldn't be. Another common thing to look for is omitted leads. It is easy to forget to connect a wire sometimes, regardless of how much experience you've had at building. When you're completely satisfied that all the wires are connected properly and nothing has been left out, start examining your solder joints.

One manufacturer of electronic kits has estimated that more than 90 percent of all malfunctioning kits can be traced to improper soldering! If you moved a joint before it had a chance to cool completely, for example, the result is what is referred to in electronics as a "cold solder joint." A cold solder joint has a fifty-fifty chance on conducting electricity **half the time!**

Fortunately, cold solder connections are fairly easy to spot most of the time. Look for a joint with a dull, grainy texture rather than a satiny metallic appearance. To be on the safe side, touch the soldering iron against each joint just long enough to make the solder flow freely once again. Don't forget to be careful with the unijunction's leads, though—it won't have built up any immunity to heat since being placed in the circuit.

After you've checked all your wiring and connections, and reheated all the joints, try the key again. If you still don't hear anything, you probably have a bad switch or a speaker with the wrong impedance. To rule out the switch or key, place a screwdriver across the contacts. But don't do it at the switch; instead, short the screwdriver across the two points where the wires from the switch tie into the circuit. If you don't hear any sound now, the problem is isolated to the speaker or the speaker wire—unless, of course, you managed to get a bad component, which is unlikely but certainly within the realm of possibility.

If you are using a speaker rather than a set of earphones, disconnect the speaker from the circuit and replace it with a 47-ohm resistor, If you don't have a pair of headphones to connect across the resistor, connect a shielded lead (with a phono plug on one end) in place of the headphones as shown in Fig. 2-12 and insert the phono plug end into any amplifier input jack , such as the auxiliary input of your stereo system. If the oscillator doesn't work now when the key is held down, you've

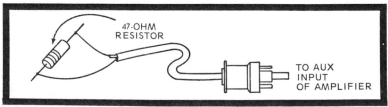

Fig. 2-12. A sure way to test your circuit is to plug it into an external amplifier.

either overlooked a wiring error or you have a bad unijunction transistor. And I'll lay my money on the unijunction because I know how well Motorola checks out their units before they send them to distributors.

If you have a voltohmmeter, check first the voltage of the battery. It should be not less than 8.5V. If that checks out all right, cut the red battery lead and place the meter in series with broken lead as shown in Fig. 2-13. Put the meter on the range that measures current, in the milliampere region. When you press the key, the meter should indicate no more than about 10 mA at most. If the reading is higher than that, you're wasting time trying to blame the unijunction because it is a sure-fire indication of a wiring error somewhere.

If you've come this far and nothing works, don't give it all up as a complete flop; at least you've had quite a bit of experience at construction, and you had the chance to do some real troubleshooting.

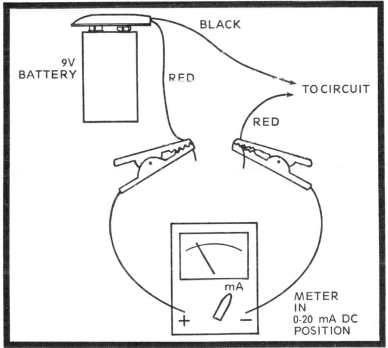

Fig. 2-13. Test setup for checking the current drain of the unijunction code practice oscillator.

Project 2

AF Signal Generator

There's always the possibility that you have no interest in becoming an amateur radio operator. And in case you already are a ham you'll not be inclined to build the code practice oscillator of the previous project. In this project we present a device whose circuit varies only slightly from that of the code practice oscillator, but it will be of little use to the novitiate, for it comes under the general classification of test equipment and is used to check out the capabilities of existing audio amplifiers.

As we go through this project, we're going to assume that you, the builder, have some experience with electronics and electronic construction, and that you would not otherwise be interested in building an audio signal generator.

USING THE AF SIGNAL GENERATOR

The "af" in the title means "audio frequency," which is the range of signals capable of being produced by the generator described here.

Although an audio generator is most useful when used in combination with an oscilloscope, the signal alone—as decoded by your own ear—can tell you many things about the audio amplifier with which it is used. It is also handy for checking the capabilities of an audio system, including the preamplifier, amplifier, and speakers. When used with a tape recorder, an audio generator greatly simplifies head alignment.

Checking Your Own Hearing Range

When used in conjunction with a good amplifier, the af signal generator can be both fun and educational, for it will test the hearing capabilities of the listeners. You will find, if you use the af signal generator when there are groups of people around, that women typically are capable of hearing sounds of higher frequency than men. And younger women are capable of hearing sounds of even higher frequency than their elders.

You can save yourself money if you're planning on purchasing a stereo system. Simply check your own personal frequency response before going into the stereo store; that is, determine the highest sound frequency that you are capable of hearing. Then, when you buy your equipment, you'll not be wheedled into buying a high-priced item whose reproduction capabilities go beyond your own hearing range.

You might be surprised to learn that your ears are totally insensitive to sounds above about 15,000 Hz. There are people who can hear all the way up to 18,000, of course, and I have even known people to hear sounds above this frequency, but not men and not people older than about 25.

At any rate, you can see the fallacy of paying for an amplifier system capable of reproducing frequencies beyond 20,000 Hz when you yourself (and most of your family and friends, most likely) can hear sounds no higher than 15,000 or 16,000. The cost of sound systems does not increase linearly with capability. Actually, a speaker capable of fairly smooth reproduction over a range of, say, 50 Hz at the low end to 15,000 Hz at the high end will be far less expensive than a speaker rated to give a flat output over the range of 50 to 20,000 Hz.

The audio generator does not have to be calibrated (to tell you the exact frequency it is producing) for you to check your hearing on a comparative basis with your friends. Simply get a pleasant note started somewhere in the middle of the audio range and start increasing the frequency gradually. If there is a group present, instruct each person to let you know when he or she is no longer hearing the sound as you continue to up the pitch of the signal.

For some reason, you'll find there are those who are ashamed to admit that they can't hear the higher frequencies—particularly those who may have a fairly large investment in high-quality sound equipment. But you can trap them easily by shutting off the sound completely when you suspect they aren't hearing the signals. If they really do hear, they'll know when you cut the signal. Similarly, they'll know when you start the signal again.

At a party, this whole process can be fun enough to be considered a game, for it seems that everyone wants to know how he hears in comparison with others.

The af signal generator does not have the output volume necessary to fill a room all by itself. So if you're going to make comparative checks, you should feed the output of the signal generator into the tape input (or auxiliary input) of an audio amplifier known to have the capability of reproducing signals beyond the range of human hearing.

Checking Tape Recorder Head Alignment

If you have only one tape recorder on hand, there is no way to align the heads properly. Of course, you can align the recording head and the playback head (if your deck has both) to track precisely together, but that is no guarantee your tapes will be playable on someone else's machine. What you really need are two machines, one of which is known to be in proper alignment already.

If you have an oscilloscope, the process will be greatly simplified because it means that you do not have to rely on your own hearing capabilities to spot discrepancies in alignment. It would also be handy to have a stereo amplifier system for coupling signals into and out of your tape deck, though this is not an actual requirement.

If you have two tape recorders handy, connect the one that is known to be in proper alignment to the "tape out" jacks of your stereo amplifier as shown in Fig. 2-14, and connect the af signal generator into the "auxiliary" mode so that the audio signal from the generator will be fed to both channels of the tape recorder. Put a fresh, clean tape on the deck and start recording with the generator putting out a signal.

If you have an oscilloscope, connect it to either speaker or to the output of the tape deck. If not, you'll have to monitor the output signal aurally from the amplifier. Increase the frequency of the generator signal until you begin to lose it with the oscilloscope (or until it gets to the threshold of

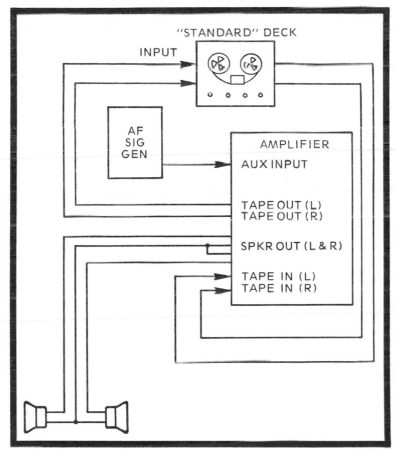

Fig. 2-14. Test setup for checking head alignment when a tape deck with properly aligned heads is available. A scope can be connected across either speaker or at the tape deck output. Set the generator for as high a frequency as you can hear. If the recorder has separate record and playback heads, monitor the output directly first, then compare with the sound obtained when the amplifier "tape monitor" switch is engaged. When both are the same, record a 10-minute test signal.

inaudibility), then back off slightly. Record the tape for at least ten minutes.

After the tape has been recorded, stop the recorder and place the recorded tape on the recorder in question. Connect the oscilloscope to the new deck's output (or monitor it with your stereo system as before). Since both channels have been recorded, change the function selector from "mono" to "stereo."

As the tape plays, the output should appear the same on the scope as it did on the "standard" recorder. And if the signal was audible on the other recorder, it should be audible now. If things aren't the same, use a screwdriver of the appropriate size to raise or lower the playback head for optimum response. When a playback head is misaligned, the high frequencies fall off before the lows, so even a slight adjustment of the head position will affect the output response of the signal.

After the signal is exactly as it should be, secure the head with epoxy around the adjustment screw. Some tape decks have special adjustment nuts to retain the positioning screws; if your machine has these, simply tighten them and forget about the epoxy.

After the playback head is properly aligned, you can use the newly adjusted head as a standard for adjusting the positioning of the record head. Start with another fresh tape using the setup you had with the "standard" recorder. As you monitor the output during record, adjust the record head for the highest-frequency output according to your ear or the scope waveform. When the waveform has the appearance of the input signal, and it is audible to the same degree, lock the record head in position and the adjustment procedure is complete.

Checking Amplifiers and Speakers

The procedure for checking an amplifier is the same as for checking a speaker. Simply feed the audio from the generator into the input of the amplifier, and listen at the speaker. To do this scientifically, you'll need a high-impedance voltmeter or an oscilloscope, for you can't trust your ears when it comes to variations in output that might not be too severe.

If you're checking the amplifier only, replace the speaker with a resistor of approximately twice the impedance value of the loudspeaker recommended for the amplifier. This will allow you to turn the volume up without blowing the minds of any listeners.

Once you have the amplifier terminated in a proper load, connect the scope's vertical input probe (directly) across the terminating resistor, and apply a signal to the amplifier input

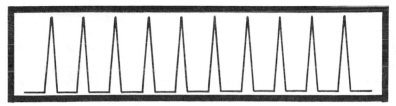

Fig. 2-15. The audio generator produces a series of pulses such as those shown here. The number of pulses per second is equal to the frequency you hear (in hertz).

from the generator. Increase the gain of the amplifier until the scope shows some distortion. The signal generator produces pulses rather than sine waves because of the characteristics of the unijunction transistor, but these pulses occurring at a periodic rate will produce the same basic sound as a sine wave at the same rate. At low frequencies, the pulses will be too far away from each other to result in a full low-frequency signal, so you'll have to restrict your testing to the amplifier's upper frequency range.

To determine what the distortion is—and to what it might be attributable—examine the input signal occasionally by connecting the scope directly to the output of the af signal generator (without disconnecting the generator from the amplifier). If your generator is functioning properly, the signal should have the appearance of the scope trace shown in Fig. 2-15. The signal, when observed at the output of the amplifier, should look exactly the same, but amplified.

Various types of possible distortion are pictured in Fig. 2-16. The first two traces are known as clipping distortion, and they indicate that the amplifier's stages are not biased properly. If the amplifier is designed well, the amplifier should clip when the input gain is increased beyond the unit's capability, but the clipping should occur on the top and the bottom of the trace simultaneously.

Amplifiers that are not linear in their reproduction capability may clip on the top at one frequency setting, then, as the pitch is increased, they may clip on the bottom half-cycles. Since this is a basic amplifier design problem, there is little that can be done short of redesigning the amplifier.

An inadequate power supply is frequently the cause of distortion in transistor amplifiers. Some signal levels may tax the power supply more than others, and when power supplies are taxed beyond their limits, they drop severely in output voltage. When the output voltage drops, the operating point of the amplifier shifts, usually lower than normal, causing excessive clipping on the lower half-cycles of the output signal.

If you've built your own amplifier, you may see output waveforms that look something like that of Fig. 2-16C, which is particularly common with complementary amplifier stages. Waveforms that show any time period between the upper half-cycle and the lower half-cycle indicate that the two output transistors are not working to their full capacity. The first half of the complementary pair in the amplifier's output will shut off before the other half begins conducting. A few resistor value changes in the output stage will correct this deficiency in most cases.

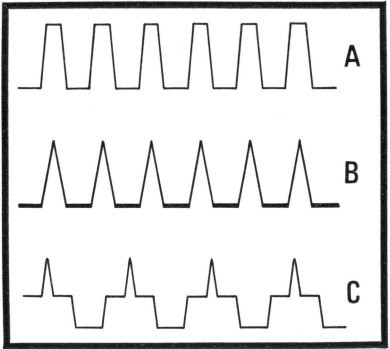

Fig. 2-16. Various waveforms showing signal distortion. At A, the amplifier is clipping the peaks off the tops of the pulses; at B, the bottom of the signal is being clipped. The indication is a heavier base line than the balance of the scope trace. At C, the output transistors are not operating to their maximum capability.

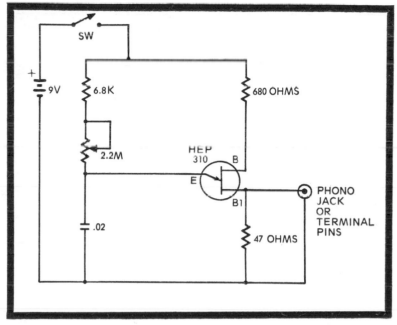

Fig. 2-17. Schematic diagram for af signal generator

BUILDING THE AF SIGNAL GENERATOR

The schematic diagram for the audio-frequency signal generator is shown in Fig. 2-17. You will notice the similarity between this unit and the code practice oscillator described in Project 1. The chief difference is the value of the trimmer potentiometer, the disc ceramic capacitor, and the fact that no speaker is to be connected to the output terminals.

The layout, of course, can be the same as that for the previous project, since the actual number and appearance of the components are identical. You should have a shielded cable, however, for connecting the signal from the generator into the input stage of the amplifier you're going to check out. Most stereo systems use "RCA"-type phono plugs, and cables are readily available at most electronic outlets. If you can't buy a PC-mount phono jack (which would allow you to use regular stereo cables), just mount a couple of push-in terminals in the board. Then, for the interconnecting cable, just cut in half one shielded cord with molded RCA plugs on each end. Of course, you'll have two cables, but you're sure to find some suitable purpose for the second length if you do much experimenting with audio circuits.

Like the previous project, you can build the af signal generator into a small plastic box. This will make the unit convenient to carry around, and will enhance its value to you as a piece of standard test equipment.

If you're skilled with the soldering iron, you might want to mount the trimmer potentiometer, switch, and phono jack on the surface of the plastic box, as shown in Fig. 2-18. This way, you can tape the box closed permanently and operate the af signal generator as if it were a regular piece of commercial test gear.

You have to change the layout from that shown in the first project, of course. And there are a few pointers you should know before mounting to the plastic.

To mount the trimmer, place the unit in the position where it will be most convenient in use. Use your thumb to press the terminals against the surface of the plastic box, then heat each

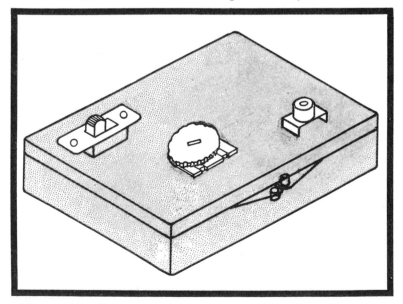

Fig. 2-18. With a little extra patience and some skill with a soldering iron, you can mount the off-on switch, the control, and the phono jack on the surface of the plastic box.

terminal with the soldering iron until the pin sinks through the plastic surface (protruding through to the underside of the box cover). Once it has been set into the plastic, it will stay because the plastic will cool around the pins and hold the device firmly in position until after you've done the soldering to the pins on the underside.

I used a slide switch rather than a toggle simply because I happened to have one around. But slide switches are cheaper than toggles, too, so that is a consideration. It is more difficult to mount a slide switch to the plastic box than it is to mount a toggle switch, but it is by no means impossible. If you're mounting a toggle switch, all you have to do is melt a hole in the box that is big enough to accept the collar bushing of the switch. But if you're mounting a slide switch, you have to use the soldering iron as if it were a saw.

The slide switch will have a couple of mounting ears for accepting mounting screws, but you won't need mounting screws if you embed the switch in the plastic. Measure the body size of the switch, which should be about ⅜ inch wide by about 1 inch long. Use a sharp object such as an awl to mark the rectangular mounting area on the box cover, then melt out the rectangular area with the tip of your soldering iron. While the plastic is still hot (after melting out the area), push the switch in firmly until the mounting ears seat against the box cover. Then just let the plastic cool. The plastic itself will do the rest. As the plastic cools, it will adhere to the body of the switch like glue.

Mounting the phono jack is just as easy. Determine the size of the jack, melt a hole, and push in the jack. You won't need any other mounting hardware.

After the external surface parts are installed, do all the board wiring. Then tape the box closed and you're in business. For storage and during transportation, there will be plenty of room inside the box to keep the interconnecting cable with its phono plugs.

Project 3

Music Instruction Metronome

If you're musically inclined, or know someone who is, you're sure to find an application for the metronome. There was a time, not too far back, when no serious piano student could be without the adjustable metronome, a springwound device that would click off the beat the student was to emulate. Times change, though. Now, most metronomes are nothing more than unijunction oscillators connected with audio amplifiers. The result is a good clean beat that is fully adjustable from a few clicks per second to as many as the fastest-handed pianist could possibly want.

As we learned at the beginning of this section, the unijunction transistor is ideally suited to applications where short beats are required because it produces pulses of extremely short duration. The sound of the metronome you can build by modifying the basic unijunction oscillator circuit remains essentially unchanged regardless of the number of beats per second you set it for.

As a matter of fact, the very accuracy of the metronome—in producing, second after second, hour after hour, the precise rate of beats that you want—makes it ideal for timing applications. One particularly good use for the unijunction metronome, for example, is in the darkroom, where clock faces are difficult to see. You can accurately gage enlarger exposures, developer immersion periods, and other timed functions, simply by counting the clicks you hear.

The parts list for the metronome is presented in Fig. 2-19. If you've built the code practice oscillator or af signal generator, you'll notice a significant difference with respect to the capacitor. Instead of loading the unijunction with a disc ceramic, the metronome requires an electrolytic capacitor.

QTY DESCRIPTION

QTY	DESCRIPTION
1	G-pattern prepunched phenolic board (Keystone Electronics No. XXXPP)
1	9V battery holder (Keystone No. 71)
1	9V battery terminal (snap-on, with leads)
2	2-56 x ¼-inch machine screws with nuts
1	Single-pole switch
1	47-ohm, ½W carbon composition resistor
1	680-ohm, ½W carbon composition resistor
1	6.8K, ½W carbon composition resistor
1	50K PC-mount trimmer potentiometer (with thumbwheel)
1	10 uF, 15V electrolytic capacitor
1	PC-mount "RCA-type" phono jack
1	HEP 310 unijunction transistor (Motorola)
1	3 ft length 22-gage hookup wire, solid Push-in terminal pins (Keystone No. 1499

Fig. 2-19. Parts list for the metronome.

For darkroom timing applications, you can follow the construction sequence described for the code practice oscillator, for the metronome does have enough output to drive a small 60-ohm speaker. However, for music instruction purposes, the audio output is insufficient, so the unit must be used with an amplifier. If you've a stereo system handy, just build up the metronome according to the schematic diagram of Fig. 2-20, and use the auxiliary input of your stereo to amplify the output of the metronome. If you keep your function selector in the "mono" position, you will hear the clicks from both sides of the stereo system.

In the event that you don't have an audio amplifier system handy, you might want to build the one shown in Fig. 2-21. It's simple and requires very few parts, and it can be built onto the same 2 x 3-inch prepunched board you used for the metronome itself. The parts list for the amplifier is shown in Fig. 2-22.

The amplifier is shown with no off-on switch because it obtains its power from the unijunction metronome circuit. When the metronome is turned on, power is applied to the amplifier, and when the unit is off, power is removed from the

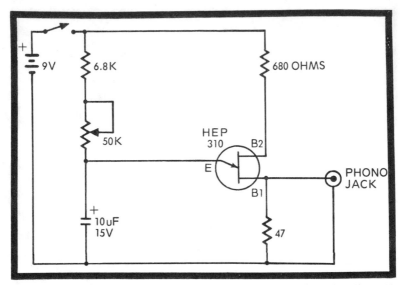

Fig. 2-20. Musical instruction metronome circuit. Adjustment of the 50K trimmer changes the beat rate of the metronome.

amplifier. Just be sure to connect the 9V amplifier power to a spot on the metronome that follows the switch. (Otherwise, the amplifier will be on all the time and battery replacement requirements will keep your pocketbook empty.)

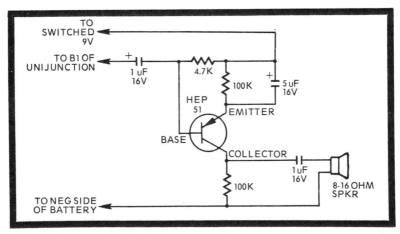

Fig. 2-21. This audio amplifier will serve nicely to up the gain of the metronome. If you have a 100K audio-taper potentiometer, you can add a volume control by replacing the collector resistor. The series capacitor feeding the speaker will then connect to the wiper arm.

QTY DESCRIPTION

2   1 uF, 15V electrolytic capacitor
1   5 uF, 15V electrolytic capacitor
I   4.7 K, ½W carbon composition resistor
2   100K, ½W carbon composition resistor
1   16-ohm speaker, high efficiency, miniature.
1   HEP51 PNP bipolar transistor
1   2 ft length 20-gage hookup wire, solid Push-in
     terminal pins (Keystone NO. 1499)

Fig. 2-22. Parts lists for the metronome amplifier.

Project 4

Signal Injector

For troubleshooting audio circuits, there is probably no piece of test equipment quite as useful as the signal injector. The key to its efficiency is the ease with which the skillful user can apply the signal at first one stage, then another, a procedure that can rapidly isolate almost any fault to the malfunctioning amplifier stage.

A signal injector must be capable of producing a tone output that is rich in harmonics if it is to be useful for any type of audio amplifier; this allows the signal to be easily coupled to stages of varying impedance characteristics, amplification factors, and input circuit loading networks.

If you are new to electronics experimentation, you might be inclined to skip over this project, opting instead for the code practice oscillator or metronome. Even if you do choose one of the other projects, you shouldn't close the door on this one, because you'll probably get more of an education from this one effort than from all the others combined. It doesn't take much "playing around" with a signal injector and a faulty amplifier to get the hang of troubleshooting. And once you develop a feel for "psyching out" problems in audio circuits, you can easily adapt the same technique to other types of circuits as well.

FINDING CIRCUIT FAULTS

Troubleshooting is about 90 percent horse sense, 8 percent knowhow, and 2 percent luck. Let us take a typical case for an example—a table model radio that doesn't work.

All you know to start with is that it "won't play." If it is a tube-type set, you know, even without a background in electronics, that when it is plugged into a convenience outlet, all the tubes should light up (when the switch is on, of course). So that's where you start. If you can't see the tubes, you remove the back of the radio so that the filaments can be viewed when the unit is plugged in. You also have to observe the construction of the radio, many are built so that when the back is removed, no power can be applied to the set. If this is the case, you have to find the safety interlock switch and defeat it when the back is removed. Remember, though, that when you do this, you must exercise extreme caution, because the open back will expose you to hazardous voltages. Your best bet is to position the radio so that you can observe all the tubes without touching the radio once it is plugged in.

The next step is to turn on the switch and plug the unit in, watching the tubes to see if they light up. Most ac-dc radios of the low-cost variety have tubes that are wired (Fig. 2-23) like a string of old-fashioned Christmas tree lights—when one goes out, they all go out. If you don't see the tell-tale flare of filaments when you plug the set in, the odds are that the set

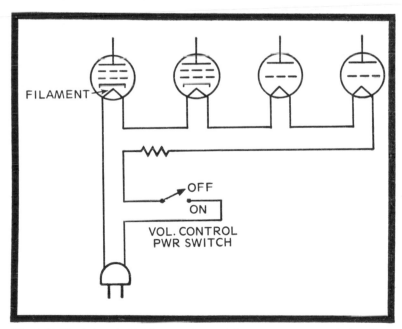

Fig. 2-23. Most "ac-dc" table-model radios have series filaments like this. You can see what happens when one of the filaments develops a break: the effect is the same as turning off the power switch. None of the tubes light because there is no complete circuit.

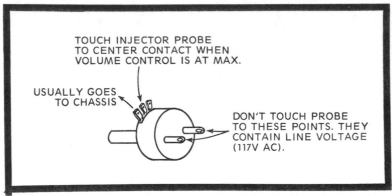

TOUCH INJECTOR PROBE
TO CENTER CONTACT WHEN
VOLUME CONTROL IS AT MAX.

USUALLY GOES
TO CHASSIS

DON'T TOUCH PROBE
TO THESE POINTS. THEY
CONTAIN LINE VOLTAGE
(117V AC).

Fig. 2-24. A shortcut to the grid of any power amplifier's input audio stage is at the volume control. Easiest way to remember which terminal is which is to always use the center pin with gain at maximum. Watch out for the high voltage on ganged volume control and power switch combinations, though; an extra pair of terminals is your clue to be careful.

has a bad tube. All you have to do in this case is unplug the set, pull out the tubes (remembering to mark which socket you pulled each tube from), and check them at your local supermarket (or the nearest place where there is a tube tester available).

If the tubes light up, though, the problem might be more serious, even though a tube could still be bad. Here's where the signal injector comes in. You can make a quick check of the audio portion of the circuit by applying a signal to the volume control wiper arm, as shown in Fig. 2-24. Be very careful here, though. Most volume controls have a set of switch contacts on the rear of the device, and the switch contacts carry household current. With the volume control turned all the way up, touch the injector probe to the center pin of the volume control. If the audio portions of the radio are performing all right, the signal will come out the speaker loud and clear. You have ruled out all but the "rf" stages of the radio. However, if the signal is not reproduced at the speaker, you'll have to start at the output and work your way toward the input methodically.

You know that you can connect your signal injector directly across a speaker and get some kind of sound, even if it isn't very loud, It follows, then, that if you couple the signal to the input of the stage that drives the speaker, you'll get a nice loud signal if the stage is amplifying properly.

To determine which tube drives the speaker, disconnect the set from the power source and remove the chassis from the radio cabinet. If you observe the area around the speaker, you will notice that the speaker is driven from a transformer, as shown in Fig. 2-25. The transformer has at least four wires; two of them go to the speaker, and the other two go to the stage that drives the speaker, either directly or indirectly.

The wires that go to the speaker are called "secondary leads" and the other wires are "primary leads." One of the primary leads may connect directly to the chassis, but the other will be coupled to the plate of the radio's final amplifier tube through a series capacitor, which serves to keep direct

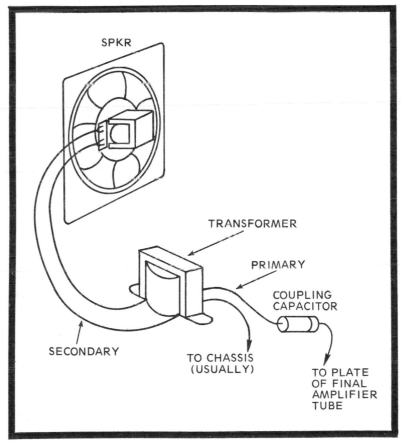

Fig. 2-25. The final amplifier can be located without a schematic just by following the electrical "path" backward from the speaker.

current from being applied to the transformer. Once you determine which tube is the final amplifier, you also know which terminal of that tube is the plate. You will want to avoid touching the plate lead because it has high-voltage direct current on it (or at least it should, if the power supply is working).

Check the plate's voltage with a voltohmmeter set for direct current, and the range switch in the 250V full-scale position. If you don't get an indication of between 200 and 230V here, the problem is probably in the power supply or rectifier; and the whole thing can be remedied by replacing the rectifier tube. If you do get a good indication of high voltage on the plate of the output stage, however, you'll have to get your signal injector and apply some audio at the grid of this tube.

If you don't have a base diagram for that particular tube, you'll have to find the grid by the process of elimination. You've already located the plate. You can now identify the filaments (two terminals) by looking for a pair of wires (usually twisted together) that connect from pins on this tube to pins on other tubes by direct connection. You can eliminate all ground points by ruling out all terminals that connect directly to the chassis. That will leave only grid leads. You can safely touch the signal injector probe to any grid lead with the radio plugged in and the volume turned up all the way. If you don't hear the signal at the speaker, you've located the faulty stage. If you do hear the signal, the faulty stage is probably the next one up the line—the one you checked when you touched the center pin of the volume control.

The volume control is connected to the grid of the first amplifier stage through a series capacitor. All you have to do is follow the wiring by observation to learn which tube serves as the initial audio amplifier.

With tube-type sets, once a fault has been isolated, a bad tube should be the first assumption. Replace the suspect tube with another of the same value if you have a spare in your junkbox. You can check the faulty-stage tube on a conventional tube tester, of course, but most commercial tube testers are notoriously inadequate for telling you much about the condition of vacuum tubes. They check emission as a rule, nothing more. So be suspicious when a tester shows a good tube in a stage that doesn't work.

The most likely thing that can go bad is a tube; next in likelihood is a burned-out resistor. Least common, fortunately, is hardest to check: a faulty capacitor used for coupling or bypassing. Burned out resistors usually leave an odor than hangs around for a long time after the set goes on the blink. Look all around the faulty stage for a resistor that has a bulge in its center; the bulge is caused by thermal expansion of the resistor's carbon content just before it blows.

Transistor amplifiers require the same, straightforward troubleshooting approach, and it is the approach used by all professionals who do electronic equipment repair for a living.

No matter how complex the audio amplifier is, troubleshooting is a simple matter, especially if you have a schematic or block diagram of the amplifier at the start. After ruling out all the logical areas, such as power supply failure, fuse breakage, etc., it is simply a matter of treating each audio stage as a complete amplifier in its own right. Always start at the stage nearest the speaker, and work your way toward the amplifier input, a stage at a time.

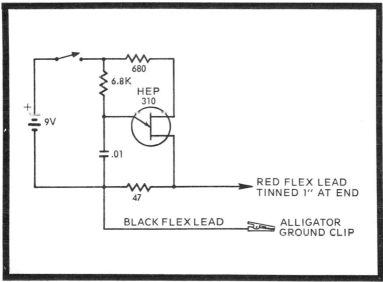

Fig. 2-26. Signal injector schematic. This is a simplification of the code practice oscillator, and does not require a variable control for tone. The two flex leads should be at least 18 inches in length.

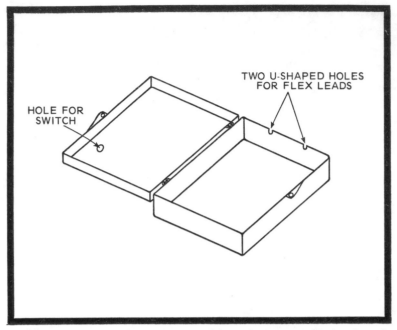

Fig. 2-27. The plastic box is prepared by using your soldering iron to "drill" one hole in the top for mounting the toggle switch and melt out two notches so the leads can be fed out while the box is closed.

SINGAL INJECTOR REQUIREMENTS

You'll recognize the basic circuit for the signal generator; it's the same unijunction oscillator we've been using in previous projects (see Fig. 2-26). The switch on the unit is a conventional single-pole, single-throw type rather than a momentary-contact type, however. This allows the signal to be turned on while the hand is free to move the probe from one stage to the next.

Another innovation is the output line. The ground side has an alligator clip at the end of an 18-inch flexible lead so that it may be conveniently connected to the common side of the audio circuit being checked. The "hot" side should be a highly flexible red conductor similar to the leads on your voltohmmeter. A probe at the end could be handy, but it isn't absolutely necessary. You can fabricate your own probe, of sorts, by simply tinning the last inch or so of the line. The solder stiffens the lead and allows it to be used as a probe.

Like the other unijunction projects, the signal injector should be built into a small container such as the plastic boxes we've used before. This construction technique makes the injector a self-contained unit and turns it into a very useful piece of test equipment.

The signal injector will be handier if it is totally enclosed but controllable from the box exterior. Thus, the power switch should be mounted on the plastic box and the two signal leads should extend out of the "cabinet," as shown in Fig. 2-27.

The switch, ideally a miniature toggle switch, can be mounted on the outside of the plastic box by using your soldering iron to melt a hole in the box large enough to accommodate the threaded switch bushing. The two leads can be fed out of the box through a pair of U-shaped notches melted from the bottom half of the box as shown in the sketch. When the injector is not in use, the two leads can be lifted from their notches and stuffed into the box for safekeeping.

Project 5

RF Signal Generator

If you built the signal injector of Project 4, this one is a must, for it is a natural "follow-on" tool that allows checkout of radio receivers of all types using the same basic troubleshooting technique of the previous project. The point is, you can check out receiver rf circuits exactly the way you check out audio circuits; simply adjust the rf generator to produce a signal of the frequency of interest to you, apply that signal to the inputs of various stages—working backward, as with the audio signal injector—and listen for an indication that the signal is not getting through. When you come to a stage where the signal doesn't get through, you've isolated the malfunctioning stage.

If you aren't intimately familiar with the workings of receivers, the intermediate frequencies, mixers, and rf amplifiers of your radio set, you'll almost have to have a schematic diagram for your radio. At the very least you'll need a block diagram.

Don't let the simplicity of the circuit shown in Fig. 2-28 fool you into thinking the rf signal generator isn't adequate for the job. While the generator won't be stable enough for precision work on communications-type receivers or radios operating on very high frequencies, it is perfect for applications involving AM broadcast radios as well as for the low i-f sections of any type receiver, FM or AM. The unijunction transistor is a particularly adaptable device, and the extremely short pulses it produces makes it well suited for rf use.

You will notice one significant difference between this circuit and those we've used for foregoing projects: The signal is tapped from a completely different spot on the oscillator.

Since a variety of radio-frequency signals will be required for checking various types of radios, you'll have to incorporate a frequency control. The value can be the same as that used for the audio generator described earlier—a 50K trimmer potentiometer. You can experiment with different values of capacitance to give you the radio-frequency range you want; I used a 0.1 uF capacitor, which allowed me to adjust the unit from the upper audio range through all the radio frequencies I might use for troubleshooting.

The output, taken from base 2 of the unijunction transistor, is a series of negative pulses that appear on an oscilloscope screen like the waveform pictured in Fig. 2-29A. This output signal should be fed to the stage under test through a series coupling capacitor with a value of about 0.01 uF, as shown in the schematic.

The construction is identical to that of the earlier unijunction circuits: the entire assembly being mounted on a G-pattern perfboard of 2 by 3 inches. The probe leads can be the same as those described for the audio signal injector: an alligator clip for the ground connection and a flexible lead tinned at the end for the probe.

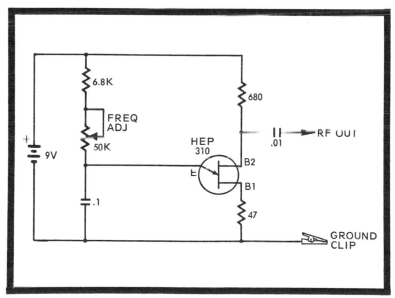

Fig. 2-28. Basic circuit for rf signal generator. Note that the output is taken from base 2 rather than base 1, and is fed through a 0.01 uF series capacitor.

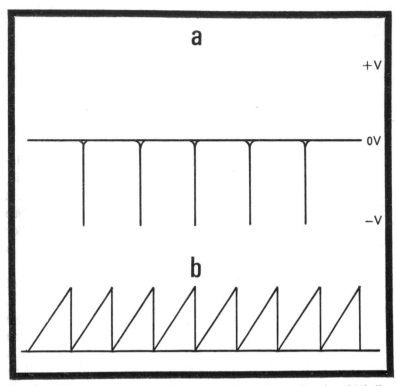

Fig. 2-29. The rf output is a series of negative-going spikes in which the repetition rate is determined by the setting of the 50K trimmer potentiometer. Sketch B shows the sawtooth waveform developed at the unijunction's emitter terminal.

A nice "side" benefit of the rf signal generator is its capability of producing waveforms other than a series of sharp spikes. At the junction of the trimmer and capacitor, for example (unijunction emitter), a sawtooth waveform (Fig. 2-29B) is developed, the frequency (or repetition rate) of which is identical to the rate of the positive pulses at base 1 and the negative pulses at base 2. If you have an oscilloscope you'll find this signal generator an extremely useful tool to have around.

Project 6
Tone-Burst Oscillator

If you aren't already a ham radio operator, if you're not involved in the business of communicating with two-way radio, if you don't have a citizens band transceiver, then this project will hold little interest for you. This project is nothing more than a simple tone oscillator, much like the one described for code practice. The chief difference is the fact that this one is not tunable and is built for precisely one frequency.

You might wonder why a tone-burst oscillator would be of interest to people who use two-way radios. Suppose, though, that you had a taxi service business that depended on the use of radio to dispatch your units. On the other side of town there might be a "ready-mix" concrete company who depends as much on radio as you do, or a construction firm with an entire fleet of radio-equipped trucks. Sometimes the FCC allows several businesses to operate on a single frequency simply because there are more applications for frequencies of operation than there are places in the radio spectrum. The result of all this would be that your taxi drivers would have to listen to the ready-mix dispatcher or the construction company's radio messages just to make sure they heard every message that you directed to them.

This is where a tone-burst oscillator comes in. If there are five businesses operating on a single frequency, there would be a continuous flood of bedlam, what with messages getting mixed up, operators not listening because they would tire of hearing the unrelated company's dispatcher. However, if each company selected a specific "entry" frequency within the audio range, they could install silencers on their receivers so that the receivers would not be able to hear any transmission other than those that bear the initial burst of tone of the proper frequency.

If your units had small tone "decoders" built into them, and these decoders responded to, say, 1950 Hz, your receiver would not allow radio signals to get to the speaker unless the 1950 Hz tone accompanied the transmitted signal. The other companies continue to use the same radio frequency, but your units never hear them, because the other companies each have their own tone-burst entry code. And, of course, they don't hear you either.

In ham radio, the deployment of repeaters is extremely popular. A repeater is a hilltop-mounted receiver that feeds all incoming signals into a high-power hilltop-mounted transmitter. A walkie-talkie can be heard by the repeater because the repeater's receiver is so well situated with respect to you. And anyone else within perhaps hundreds of miles can hear the signal after the repeater gets through retransmitting it from its ideal vantage point.

Some hams don't like the idea of their signals being repeated, though. They want to operate without the assistance of any automatic machinery. So, to please everyone, the repeater owners install tone-burst decoders at the repeater site. There, the only signals that get repeated are those of stations who want their signals to have the special "assist" offered by the automatic repeater. It then becomes the responsibility of the individual user to determine whether or not he will take advantage of the services the repeater affords. If he wants to use the repeater, he must install a simple tone-burst oscillator in his transmitter.

The first requirement in using a tone-burst system is to determine what that burst frequency is. It may be anywhere between 1500 and 3000 Hz, and if your oscillator is not within 20 or 30 Hz of the proper frequency, it won't trigger the decoder with which it is related.

The second requirement is to be absolutely certain that your tone-burst oscillator is set to operate on the proper frequency, regardless of temperature, humidity, and other environmental factors. This is the hard part. Capacitors are notoriously temperature sensitive; the values tend to change with the ambient temperature of their environment. Resistors change, too, though not as much. With resistors, the worst offenders are the variable types.

Some manufacturers make capacitors of materials that are specially designed to hold to their rated values in spite of environmental conditions. Mylar capacitors, for example, are particularly stable; they cost more, too. For the tone-burst oscillator shown in Fig. 2-30, we use a precision resistor and a Mylar capacitor. These two precautions should serve as assurance that the output tone will stay the same, no matter where the radio transmitter is mounted and regardless of the weather.

The only suggestion with respect to building the oscillator is to use a variable trimmer resistor at the outset. As soon as the oscillator has been trimmed to the exact frequency of operation, the value of the trimmer should be measured and the unit replaced with a fixed resistor whose tolerance of error is 1 percent.

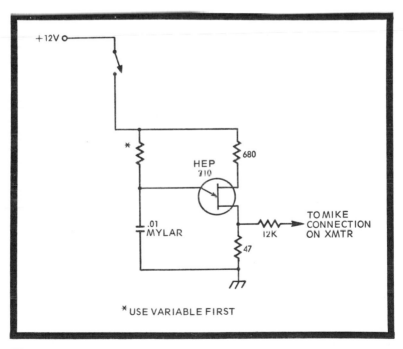

Fig. 2-30. Tone-burst schematic. For stability, the emitter capacitor should have a Mylar dielectric. The resistor marked with the asterisk should be a variable at the outset; when the oscillator is tuned to frequency, the variable can be replaced with a close-tolerance fixed resistor.

If the tone-burst oscillator is to be used in a mobile unit, you won't need to incorporate a battery because there will be adequate power available within the radio unit itself. If it's a tube-type unit, you'll have 12V handy as filament power, and if it's a transistor rig, it operates on the car's battery voltage. Thus, the oscillator can be built on a very tiny piece of perfboard and neatly inside the transmitter itself. All you'll have to do is find a convenient place to mount the push-button (the control head of an FM two-way unit is ideal).

Simple Field-Effect
Transistor Circuits

One of the most fascinating solid-state devices ever to be discovered is the field-effect transistor, known universally by the acronym "FET." The principal reason FETs are fascinating is that they closely resemble vacuum tubes in operating characteristics. Ordinary bipolar transistors are markedly different from tubes—they are current amplifiers, in general, rather than voltage amplifiers. They typically have a relatively low input impedance and a very low output impedance. But not the FET; the FET can very often be used to replace a vacuum tube in a circuit with no more modification than eliminating the original vacuum tube's filament supply. The FET's input impedance may be anywhere from 10 megohms or so to hundreds of megohms. And the output impedance is just high enough to match the input requirements of an ordinary transistor.

What this means to the builder of electronic circuits is simplicity. It means that elaborate matching networks—transformers and resistive circuitry—can be eliminated entirely, simply by choosing the circuit components so that FETs are used where high-impedance characteristics are required and bipolar transistors are used in output circuits, where low impedances are more desirable.

There are two basic field-effect transistor types—the junction device and the insulated-gate device. The junction devices are somewhat easier to work with than the other type, so we'll be working exclusively with them. Insulated-gate FETs, often called MOSFETs (for metal-oxide semiconductor field-effect transistor), are a little tricky; a wrong touch at the wrong time causes irreparable damage. And since the insulated-gate FET is inherently more expensive than the junction FET, it seems sounder to go the junction route with circuits that work equally well with either type.

LEARNING ABOUT FETs

The field-effect transistor is sufficiently different from the bipolar transistor that it has its own schematic symbol, as shown in Fig. 3-1. It has three electrodes, just like the bipolar, and the three electrodes have functions that are similar to the functions of the bipolar's base, emitter, and collector; but the internal structure differs considerably.

The junction FET is so named because of its single positive-negative junction. Diode—and unijunction transistors, too—also have single p-n junctions, but the FET's junction is usually circumferential, as shown in Fig. 3-2. The FET is a bar of either negatively or positively doped silicon, into which impurities of the opposite polarity are imposed in such a manner as to form a channel of one polarity surrounded by a field of the other. The figure shows the most common arrangement, an n-channel FET.

The operation of the FET can be likened to a garden hose with water flowing through it. When you squeeze the hose, the water passing through is restricted—less volume passes the strictured point in a given time period. When a high potential (of negative polarity for an n-channel FET) is applied to the gate, the "hose" is squeezed, and only a small amount of current is allowed to flow; when the voltage is reduced, the channel widens and current flows through easily.

ADVANTAGES OF THE FET

The operation of the FET is so simple and straightforward that it can almost make you wonder why they aren't used more extensively than transistors. The fact is, if bipolar transistors had not been discovered until after the FET, the FET would very likely be the key semiconductor today, for the FET is the perfect answer to many of the bipolar's short-comings. But the FET didn't come first, so improvements and innovations in FET technology have been slow by comparison, and the FET does have inherent shortcomings of its own. The limited power-handling capability is the FET's classic stumbling block. Where a bipolar transistor can today be used to deliver tremendous amounts of power directly into a loudspeaker (for example), the FET is still generally available only for low-signal jobs. And it takes several FETs to yield an amplification-factor figure of a single bipolar transistor.

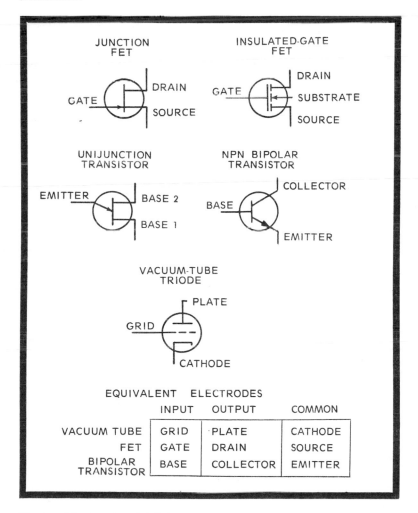

EQUIVALENT ELECTRODES

	INPUT	OUTPUT	COMMON
VACUUM TUBE	GRID	PLATE	CATHODE
FET	GATE	DRAIN	SOURCE
BIPOLAR TRANSISTOR	BASE	COLLECTOR	EMITTER

Fig. 3-1. The junction FET has three terminals and is similar in many respects to other amplifiers. Yet, it is different in principle of operation and structure, so it has its own special symbols.

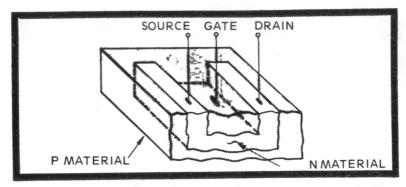

Fig. 3-2. The n-channel FET is a silicon slab whose ends are doped with n-type impurities. A narrow channel of the n material connects the two ends. The channel is surrounded by p-impurity silicon. In most circuits, the symmetry of the FET is such that the device can be reversed, allowing source to be used for drain and vice versa.

Nonetheless, the high input impedance and the moderate-to-low output impedance of the FET keeps it untouchable as an early-stage amplifier. The business of signal amplification is based on proper matching of impedances. Where the input impedance of an amplifier is the same as the characteristic impedance of the incoming signal's circuit, the signal may be coupled directly to the amplifier stage. When the impedance levels do not match, the signal must be modified to make it acceptable by the stage.

Take a crystal microphone, for example, with an impedance of several tens of thousands of ohms. It can be coupled directly into a vacuum tube, because a vacuum tube's input impedance is also quite high (actually mugh higher than the microphone). It can be coupled directly into the FET, too. But the bipolar transistor's input impedance is so low that a transformer must be used between the microphone and the amplifier.

Now, take that same amplifier and couple it to a speaker, whose characteristic impedance is low—no more than a few ohms. The tube's output impedance is far too high, so a transformer must be used. What we gained on the input, we have lost on the output. A bipolar transistor can be made to couple directly into a speaker; but what we've gained here, we lost at the input. The FET's output impedance is too high, too, not to mention the fact that a speaker's power requirements would more than likely be more than our FET could handle.

The smart circuit designer takes all these things into consideration, and employs just the right devices all the way down the line. He knows that the more components he cab eliminate, the better his circuit will be. Where a high input impedance is required, he'll use a bipolar transistor. It just so happens that the output impedance of the FET matches extremely well with the input requirements of the bipolar transistor. So he'll start with a FET, couple the signal from the FET into a bipolar stage, and go right into his low-impedance load. No transformers, no special networks—just good circuit design with a minimum of complexity.

CONSTRUCTION PRECAUTIONS

Like any other semiconductor, the FET must be handled with a reasonable amount of care until it's safely in the circuit. Insulated-gate FETs require a great deal more care than junction FETs, but since we won't be doing any building with insulated-gate FETs, we'll ignore their precircuit weaknesses. Remember that the FET is heat sensitive and can be destroyed by excessive temperature during the soldering operation, and you should do all right. If you haven't read the general precautions for semiconductors, presented in an earlier chapter, make it a point to study them before using the FET in a circuit.
detail on lead length. The input circuit impedance of the FET is very high, which makes the wires in this area particularly susceptible to noise pickup. If you keep your leads short and direct, though, you shouldn't have any trouble in this regard.

Project 7

Hi-Fi Phono Preamplifier

An excellent way to witness the remarkable high-impedance amplification properties of the field-effect transistor is to build the single-FET amplifier circuit shown in Fig. 3-3. As you can see by looking over the schematic, there really isn't much to it. But there needn't be, for the FET is ideally suited to the natural character of the crystal or ceramic phono cartridge's output, and the output of the FET is an excellent match for a pair of high-impedance headphones (2000 ohms or so).

In this simple amplifier, the FET's gate is biased by the 2.2M resistor, and the source is biased by the 4.7K resistor. The 50 uF electrolytic capacitor from source to ground provides a short circuit for audio frequencies, which makes the source common with respect to both gate and drain. This configuration of amplifier is called "common source." and offers the highest gain of any of the three basic amplifier configuration of amplifier is called "common source," and gate). The common-source FET amplifier's nearest bipolar equivalent circuit is the common-emitter; the nearest vacuum-tube equivalent is the common-cathode arrangement.

The output is fed through the wiper arm of the series-connected 10K drain potentiometer, which serves as a volume control. The 10 uF electrolytic capacitor in the output line allows audio frequencies to pass, but blocks off the direct current that would otherwise pass through from the circuit's battery supply.

ACQUIRING THE PARTS

The simplicity of this unit allows extreme miniaturization. I built the unit on the same 2 x 3 inch perforated phenolic board that I used for my unijunction oscillator because I happened to have a few extra pieces of it lying around after completing the earlier projects. But I needn't have used a piece even that big. The battery takes up more space than any of the other components; if you "build in" the 9V battery, you'll find that an ordinary transistor battery, with its holder, takes up nearly half the 2 x 3-inch space. The use of a board this size is recommended, though, even if it does leave you with some extra room; you can use that leftover space to mount an additional amplifier stage, and thus get enough volume to drive a loudspeaker to respectable volume.

I like this particular circuit because it has something special to offer besides miniaturization: high fidelity. With this preamplifier, you get a frequency response that is probably a good deal better than your headphones themselves are capable of. And the add-on amplifier stage, which is described later, won't compromise this response in the least. The following paragraphs describe the components used in the phono preamplifier. (See Fig. 3-4 for complete parts list.)

The Basics

What I call "basics" are those components that do not contribute directly to the performance of the amplifier but which are required in the actual construction. These include

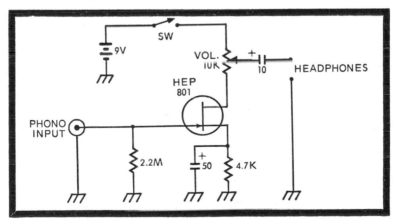

Fig. 3-3. The simple field-effect transistor preamplifier provides enough gain to drive a pair of headphones (2000 ohms or so) to a very respectable level. The power switch (SW) can be part of the volume control (10K, audio taper); be sure to mention it when you buy the parts.

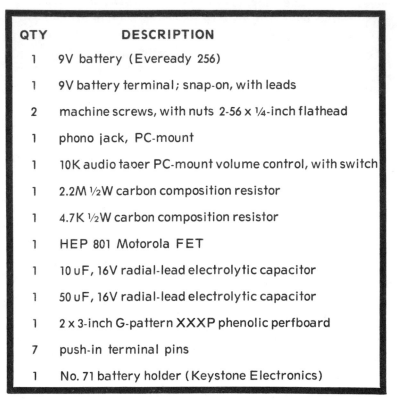

QTY	DESCRIPTION
1	9V battery (Eveready 256)
1	9V battery terminal; snap-on, with leads
2	machine screws, with nuts 2-56 x ¼-inch flathead
1	phono jack, PC-mount
1	10K audio taoer PC-mount volume control, with switch
1	2.2M ½W carbon composition resistor
1	4.7K ½W carbon composition resistor
1	HEP 801 Motorola FET
1	10 uF, 16V radial-lead electrolytic capacitor
1	50 uF, 16V radial-lead electrolytic capacitor
1	2 x 3-inch G-pattern XXXP phenolic perfboard
7	push-in terminal pins
1	No. 71 battery holder (Keystone Electronics)

Fig. 3-4. Phono preamplifier parts list.

the perfboard (2 x 3 inch, which you can cut from a larger piece), battery holder, snap-on battery terminal (with leads), push pins, phono jack, wire, nuts and bolts, etc.

Wire. You won't need much wire for this project—only a couple of inches. For most of the component interconnections, the wires on the components themselves are of sufficient length to preclude the necessity of cutting more for linking. Figure 3-5 shows the layout I used, which I especially recommend for experimenters who are new to the field of electronics. Notice that only one length of wire is used, other than that of the battery terminal smap, and this wire is used as a common grounding bus. When you cut component leads, always save the cut-off pieces; it often happens that these small lengths are ideal for very short wire runs.

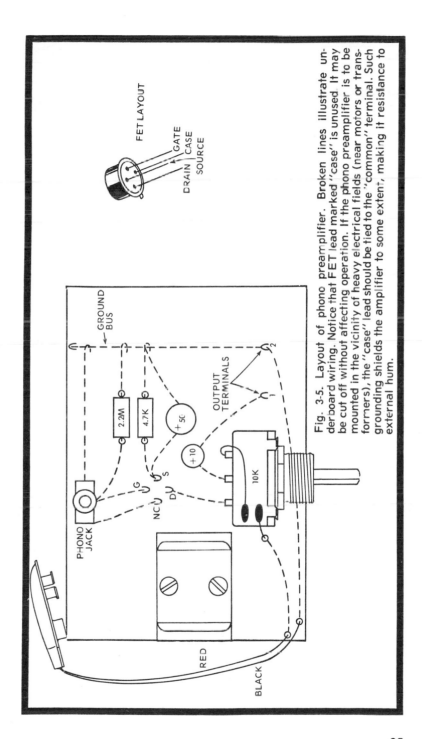

Fig. 3-5. Layout of phono preamplifier. Broken lines illustrate underboard wiring. Notice that FET lead marked "case" is unused. It may be cut off without affecting operation. If the phono preamplifier is to be mounted in the vicinity of heavy electrical fields (near motors or transformers), the "case" lead should be tied to the "common" terminal. Such grounding shields the amplifier to some extent, making it resistance to external hum.

GROUND BUS

2.2M

4.7K

+ 5c

OUTPUT TERMINALS

+ 10

10K

PHONO JACK

G

S

NC

D

RED

BLACK

FET LAYOUT

GATE
CASE
DRAIN
SOURCE

Push Pins. The push-in terminals are the Keystone 1499 type, available at most electronic parts distributors in bags of 100. The layout shown in Fig. 3-5 depicts seven of these, but you can dispense with one of them easily (the one FET terminal labeled "NC"). The terminal pins aren't easy to push into the holes of the G-pattern board, as you've already discovered if you've been building some of the projects described earlier. If you've managed to gain a little proficiency in the handling of your long-nose pliers, though, you shouldn't have any trouble inserting the terminals. Just grip each pin securely with the pliers and press firmly into the hole. If you squeeze a little too tight, the pin will close, but a small screwdriver is all it takes to open it again.

Try to orient the pins as shown in the sketch; that is, so the openings on the tops are all more or less uniform. It tends to simplify the underboard wiring and makes for a neater overall construction job than would otherwise result.

Battery Holder and Hardware. If you use the same battery holder I used (Keystone 71), you'll need two 2-56 machine screws and nuts to mount it. If you can't get the screws in a length of 1/3 or 3 |8 inch, you can always use a longer one, then "dike off" the excess with your wirecutters. The only important thing to remember about the screws is that you want flat-head or pan-head types. A round-head or panel-mount countersunk head will stick up into the holder too far and you'll have trouble seating the battery.

The battery holder mounting holes won't line up perfectly with the holes in the phenolic board, but a very small amount of reaming with a tiny-blade screwdriver will take care of that problem easily.

Phono Jack. The phono jack should be an "RCA" type. Actually, RCA has little to do with these jacks; the name probably stems from RCA's initial use of this configuration. The jack is the same type found in the rear of virtually any stereo amplifier today. If you're shopping for the parts in a local electronics outlet, be sure to specify "printed circuit mounting," or there will be no telling what you'll end up with. If your electronic outlet doesn't carry PC-mount phono jacks, you can order them direct from Hitron Semiconductors, 841 Merrick Road, Baldwin, N.Y. 11510. The model number is K1RCA; they're sold ten per bag, two dollars, postpaid.

I always use PC-mount phono jacks because they are extremely easy to mount, both on the phenolic perfboard and on plastic parts boxes. The pins of the jack line up perfectly with the G-pattern holes of the board, so mounting is simply a matter of reaming out one hole large enough to accommodate the plug, then inserting the jack assembly right onto the board. Mounting on plastic is just as easy: Just heat the phono jack terminal pins with a soldering iron and it will melt right into the box. When the melted plastic hardens, the jack is mounted securely.

Snap-On Battery Terminal You shouldn't have any trouble at all getting this item. Most parts stores carry at least one line of them, though chances are you'll have to buy a bag of five or ten. Don't hesitate to do it. If you get involved in miniature work of any magnitude at all, you'll go through these at a pretty rapid rate. If you have everything you need already but can't get to the store for this item, you can "borrow" one from that little transistor radio you've got lying around that doesn't work any more.

Phenolic Prepunched Board. I always use Keystone G-pattern XXXP here, but it isn't always easy to find. Such boards are sold by almost every electronics distributor, but it appears under a wide variety of brand names, the most popular of which is Vector. The numbering system of all the distributors is similar, though, so if you simply ask for G-pattern XXXP prepunched phenolic board, you'll get it. If you have trouble finding it locally, you may order it from Newark (and probably a number of other major mail-order outlets).

The Field-Effect Transistor

The FET is a small-signal type that is manufactured and distributed by Motorola Semiconductor Products Co. The HEP 801 is probably the most popular little FET in the company's hobby-experimenter line. You shouldn't have any trouble finding it in your local electronics store; most such stores keep a fairly complete inventory of the more popular "HEP" semiconductors. If you can't get it, though, do drop a line to Motorola Semiconductor Products Corp., HEP Sales Div., Scottsdale, Arizona. If you don't get the device directly from the manufacturer, at least you'll get a letter telling you where you can find what you're looking for.

Even though the circuit for the phono preamplifier was designed by Motorola, and especially to suit the requirements of the HEP 801, you should know that there isn't anything magic about that particular FET. You should have no trouble at all substituting any other small-signal FET that meets the same basic parametric criteria. If your local dealer can't supply you with the HEP 801, odds are he'll be able to supply you with a perfectly suitable substitute of a competitor's manufacture.

Capacitors

Both capacitors in this circuit are electrolytic types. You should try to get them with a rated working voltage of 15 or 16V, if possible. If you get electrolytic capacitors with a much higher working-voltage rating, the values at 9V may be considerably different from those specified on the electrolytic cases.

Electrolytics, as we noted early in this book, are supplied in two styles: radial-lead or axial-lead. For printed-circuit work, which is what we're simulating with the perforated phenolic board construction, the radial-lead electrolytic is best. It takes up far less space on the board because both the device's leads extend from one end of the capacitor. This allows you to stand the unit up on the board vertically so that both leads feed directly into the board. There is nothing wrong with axial-lead devices, of course; it's just that they require horizontal mounting, which consumes precious space.

Switch and Volume Control

You will notice that no switch is shown in the pictorial diagram of the wired unit (Fig. 3-5). This is because the switch is actually part of the volume control. If you look at the control in the sketch, you will see that there are five contacts on the back. The three in-line terminals are connections to the volume control proper; the other two represent the power switch.

Volume controls with integral switches are extremely common, and you'll have no trouble finding one anywhere. Unfortunately, however, there are myriads of configurations of such switch-controls. You won't have any problem if you remember that somewhere on the control there will be three terminals in a straight line, and somewhere else on the control will be two terminals alone. The two terminals will be those of the switch. The three will be the control. The center terminal in the group of three will be the wiper arm (shown as an arrow on the schematic diagram of Fig. 3-3).

CONSTRUCTION

Your layout will depend to a large extent on the configuration of the volume control and switch combination, since this is perhaps the part with the greatest possibility of size variation. If your volume control is the PC-mounting type, it will probably plug right into the board as shown in Fig. 3 5; if not, however, your layout will probably differ from the one pictured. At any rate, once provisions have been made for accommodating the control, the rest of the mounting should be duck soup.

You will notice that the layout shown allows plenty of space for installation of the battery holder, which has to contain the 9V transistor-radio battery we use for the power source. Don't let your volume control eat up space that will ultimately be required by the battery after it is installed in the holder.

Mount the battery holder after determining the volume-control requirements. Put the holder in the position where you intend to mount it and draw circles on the board using the battery holder's screw holes as a pattern. Then use a reamer or small screwdriver to ream out the circled holes on the board so that the machine screws will pass easily through them.

The next step is the phono jack. Mount it as close to the battery holder as you can while making sure you still have plenty of room for access to both the jack and the battery when the unit is completed. PC-mounting phono jacks have slightly curved mounting pins that must be straightened with your long-nose pliers before they will push easily into the board holes. Ream out the hole where the center pin of the jack will go so that the entire length of the phono plug can be accommodated when the unit is completed. After the phono jack is mounted, bend the two mounting pins over on the underboard slightly to hold the jack in place during the subsequent soldering operations.

The push-in terminal pins are next. Try to get them in as close to the positions pictured (Fig. 3-5) as you can. Don't worry about squeezing the ends with the long-nose pliers; these pins can readily be opened again with a screwdriver after they're all installed. For neatness, make sure you get them oriented in the same general direction as shown (all openings point the same way).

Bend the leads of the two resistors at right angles immediately adjacent to their bodies, and push the leads down through the board holes as shown. On the underboard side, bend the leads a bit to hold them in place. Then insert the leads of the two radial-lead electrolytic capacitors so that when they are in the board the positive leads are oriented as shown. Bend these leads over on the underboard side, too.

After you solder in a short length of bare wire for the bus bar, the rest of the soldering operation is simple. The actual point-to-point wiring is shown by broken lines in the sketch of Fig. 3-5.

The last thing to do in any electronic construction project is to install the semiconductors. In this case, of course, there is only one—the field-effect transistor. Treat it kindly and remember to heatsink the leads with the long-nose pliers when you solder them. Observe the FET layout diagram to make sure you don't transpose the leads. If you're using the Motorola HEP 801, the little identifying protrusion on the outer rim of the transistor case marks the drain lead, although it is actually placed between the drain and the lead that connects to the case of the transistor.

The case probably doesn't need to be connected at all; however, it is usually best to connect it to a ground because that serves to shield the insides of the semiconductor against any possible hum that might be caused by stray radiation fields, such as nearby electrical wires and the like.

TESTING

The best way to test the preamplifier is by connecting a low level signal to it and plugging the output of the unit directly into a power amplifier. If you have a crystal- or ceramic-cartridge phonograph handy, plug the leads from the cartridge directly into the phono jack of your preamplifier and attach a pair of high-impedance headphones to the preamplifier's output terminals.

If things don't work out exactly right—if the volume control doesn't give you increased gain as you turn it clockwise—doublecheck your wiring, the polarities of the electrolytic capacitors, and the individual leads on the FET. If the volume control gives you full output when the control is adjusted to nearly the fully counterclockwise position, you have the leads reversed on the three-pin group. Simply exchange the leads on the two outer pins of the control and the problem should disappear.

It almost goes without saying, of course, that your battery has to be up to par for you to enjoy the benefits of any amplifier. If you have a voltmeter handy, check the battery voltage while the volume control is in the maximum-volume position (and the switch on). The voltage should not drop to less than 8.5V during this test. If it drops to just slightly less than this, the problem is probably that you are using the wrong impedance value of headphones. If it drops to a fraction of the proper voltage, there is a short (or partial short) in your wiring, and you must recheck everything all over again.

ADDING AN AMPLIFIER

It could be that the preamplifier is an unsatisfactory solution to your problem of getting loud music from a crystal phono cartridge. In this case, you easily add an additional stage and use the amplifier to drive a speaker. It won't be

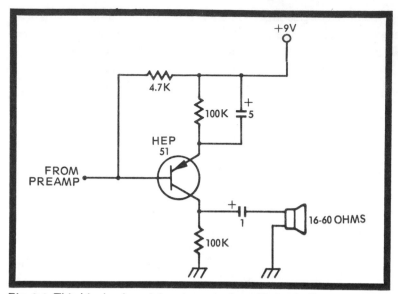

Fig. 3-6. This bipolar-transistor stage can be added onto the same board as the FET preamp, and will provide amplification enough to drive a small speaker.

room-filling by any means, but it will relieve you of the drag of having to wear headphones every time you want to listen to records.

Figure 3-6 shows a schematic diagram for a simple one-transistor amplifier stage that can fit right onto the preamplifier you've already built—assuming, of course, that you managed to leave a little extra space on the board.

The output impedance of a bipolar stage is quite low, but it isn't really as low as it needs to be to drive a speaker of the 4- to 8-ohm class. The amplifier will operate with loads of this low impedance, but the gain will be less than it would be if the load were somewhat higher, say from 16 to 60 ohms or so. Most intercom speakers will work very well with this circuit; they have a typical impedance value of 45 ohms, which makes them extremely useful for most transistor-amplifier circuits. The complete parts list is presented in Fig. 3-7.

Figure 3-8 shows the add-on amplifier mounted to the preamplifier board. It is extremely important to mount the new components so that their leads do not interfere with the wires already installed and positioned. The layout shown depicts all components actually straddling the ground bus,

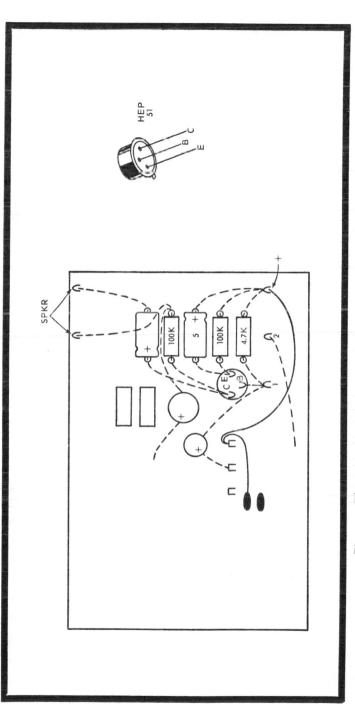

Fig. 3-8. The add-on amplifier's parts are inserted directly over the ground bus traversing the underboard. Labeled parts are new; unlabeled components are part of preamplifier.

93

which traverses the board on the underside. This being the case, not all leads will be able to be fed on the underside. Those leads pictured solid in the sketch are to be wired on the **component** side of the board. If you attempt to put the leads under the board, the wiring will be very tight, and you're almost certain to run into interference problems.

To help you know which component is which, those in Fig. 3-8 that are labeled are the new components; those unlabeled represent the components that were already wired. Another interesting point is that until now all electrolytics were radial-lead types. However, to allow us to straddle the ground bus without encumbrances, we must now use a couple of axial-lead electrolytics, as pictured.

You need five additional push-in terminals: three for the transistor, one for the battery voltage, and one for the speaker output. Start by placing the push-in terminals in their proper positions. Then bend the resistor leads in the same manner as you did for the preamplifier, and insert them into the board as shown. Be sure to leave ample space between the two 100K resistors (color coded brown, black, and yellow) so your 5 uF electrolytic capacitor will fit. But don't wire in the capacitors yet, since their leads will be at least partially on the com-

QTY	DESCRIPTION
1	4.7K ½W carbon composition resistor
2	100K ½W carbon composition resistor
1	1 uF, 16V electrolytic capacitor (axial leads)
1	5 uF, 16V electrolytic capacitor (axial leads)
5	push-in terminal pins (Keystone 1499)
1	Motorola HEP 51 pnp transistor
1	moderate-impedance speaker (16-60 ohms)

Fig. 3-7. Parts list for the add-on amplifier.

ponent side of the board. Connect a short bare wire between the pin marked B (base) and output terminal 1, but don't solder it yet. Connect the adjacent 4.7K resistor lead to terminal 1 also, then apply solder to hold both leads.

Now, bend the leads of the 5 uF capacitor and push them down into the board holes so the device is situated approximately as shown. If the leads on the underside are clear of already installed wiring, bring the positive lead of the capacitor into contact with the outer lead of the lower 100K resistor and the remaining lead of the new 4.7K resistor, and solder them to the newly inserted pin marked with the plus sign. Wrap the negative lead of the 5 uF electrolytic and the remaining lead of the 100K resistor together and solder to the transistor pin marked E (emitter).

Solder the outermost lead of the remaining 100K resistor to the ground bus on the underboard side, and solder the positive lead of the 1 uF electrolytic to the outermost speaker terminal as shown. This leaves two leads unconnected.

The free end of the 100K resistor should now be soldered to the transistor pin marked C (collector). The last connection requires care because of the new abundance of wires. Bring the negative lead of the 1 uF electrolytic across on the top side of the board, then push it down through so that it makes contact with the 100K resistor lead that ties to the collector terminal. If it touches no other leads, neither on the bottom of the board nor the underside, solder it in place.

If you now connect a short length of insulated wire between the power switch and the "plus" the unit will be ready to test.

Project 8
Four-Input Audio Mixer

If you play a musical instrument, sing with a group, or both, this project should be very appealing. It's simple enough for you to complete easily in one evening, yet complete enough to give you a valuable—and quite expensive, if you had to buy it—recording tool.

One of the biggest headaches of tape-recording small musical groups is getting loudness levels set just right. Indeed, in my own early days of electronics, I used to spend fully half the recording period trying to balance the audio for the various guitars, drummers, and singers. Without a recording studio, the problems are manifold: If you have a mike before a singer, that mike hears the music blasted from the guitar amplifiers as much as it does the voice. But turning down the guitar amplifier causes other problems because the guitar player now can't hear his own instrument sufficiently. And the more amplifiers there are in a group, the harder it is to achieve an ultimate balance.

Just when you're sure you have things exactly right, one of the instrumentalists will hit it a little harder than he should and the VU meter on the recorder will go into the red zone, indicating severe distortion, and you'll have to start the "take" from scratch.

While not the perfect solution, an audio mixer is probably the most efficient and logical answer, particularly if the "recording engineer" is not actually playing one of the instruments or singing with the group.

If there are no singers in the group, and the music is 100 percent instrumental, the operation is simplified: The instruments all go into the mike mixer rather than into their own individual amplifiers. If you want a stereo recording, of

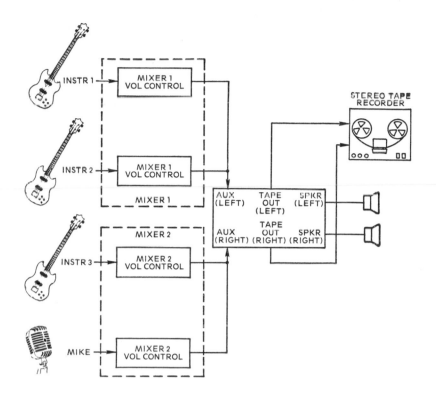

Fig. 3-9. If two mixers are used with a conventional stereo system, professional recordings can readily be made because stereo sound adjustments don't affect the signal appearing on the tape itself.

course, you should use two of the mixers, even though you may not use all of the inputs to both channels.

A good, fairly high-powered stereo system in your living room offers another huge advantage for professional home recordings, for the amplifiers can be used to monitor what goes onto the tape without interfering with the music in any way. Figure 3-9 shows how the system is interconnected. The instruments are fed to the audio mixer (two for stereo, remember), and the mixer is fed into the auxiliary input of the stereo amplifier. The tape recorder gets its input from the stereo system's tape out jacks. This way, the bass, treble, and volume controls of the stereo system can be adjusted for best room reproduction without affecting the material going onto the tape. The tape out gets its signal from the stereo ahead of the bass, treble, and volume controls, so that no matter what anyone does to the controls, there will be no interaction with the recorded program.

The fellow in charge of the tape recording will have to wear headphones; otherwise, he'll not be able to distinguish between the program going onto the tape and the music being amplified and played through the stereo amplifiers. In the recording studio, of course, the recording engineers are enclosed within a soundproof cubicle. The musicians are often allowed to turn the individual controls of the playback apparatus to any setting they prefer because of the noninterference between these controls and the signal to be recorded. The engineer, though, should have the capability of monitoring the signal actually being recorded. Naturally, this approach is far superior when a tape recorder with multiple heads is employed. (The existence of separate record and playback heads allows the engineer to monitor what is already recorded no more than a split-second after the signal is impressed onto the tape.)

To properly set the volume controls on the mixer (or mixers, if the program is to be recorded in stereo), the recording engineer initially runs a length of test tape, at which time he asks all the instrumentalists to play simultaneously at their maximum volume level. This test should be done while the tape recorder's input level controls are set at their normal position. The engineer then starts adjusting the individual volume controls of the mixer while monitoring with earphones.

It is much more efficient to dispense with one of the two channels of the stereo system while making this initial setup adjustment, either by keeping one of the recording level controls set at minimum or by keeping the second audio mixer turned off while the first one is being adjusted.

When a proper musical balance of instruments for one channel is determined, and the mixer controls set accordingly, the second channel is set up similarly. Ideally, all instruments should be heard in good proportion to the whole of the music, but the overall signal level at the tape recorder input should not exceed zero decibels (the spot where the VU meters mark maximum undistorted input).

Once the mixer and recorder controls are set, the test tape can be played back for the musicians to see if there is consensus about the input sound mix. Then it's time to remove the test tape, put in the blank fresh reel, and start recording for real.

The entire process takes a great deal longer than you might think—sometimes several hours. The chief problem is that there are usually several people to be satisfied: the leader of the group, the individual instrumentalists, and the recording engineer. By the time the recording positions satisfy everyone, the musicians are thoroughly exhausted and the engineer is probably ready to swear off recording forever. On later playback, however, nobody will regret anything because the results will show that every ounce of effort spent in preparation paid off.

THE CIRCUIT

The schematic diagram for the four-input audio mixer is presented in Fig. 3-10. As shown, the four individually controlled inputs are fed to the gate of a Motorola HEP 801 field-effect transistor through 100K input series resistors. The output impedance of the FET is ideal for matching the input requirements of the unity-gain bipolar transistor, an emitter follower which offers an output impedance that is low enough to match virtually any power amplifier and ideal for coupling to tape recorders.

CONSTRUCTION CONSIDERATIONS

The construction concept is similar to that employed in previous projects in this book; that is, the entire assembly is built onto a perfboard "chassis," and enclosed in a standard plastic parts box. Since it is advantageous to have the input and output jacks, as well as the level controls, accessible from outside the box, these are mounted on the plastic box as shown in Fig. 3-11.

The phono jacks are the same type used in Project 7. When mounting them, try to make sure they are all lined up on the back of the box as shown. The output jack should be separated from the inputs so it can be easily distinguished from them in use. You should also remember to leave enough space between the group of four jacks so that plugging and unplugging of inputs can be accomplished easily without interference from the other inputs.

The plastic parts box is comprised of two identical halves, and these can be separated by carefully snapping them apart. It is a good idea to work on the box while it is two separate

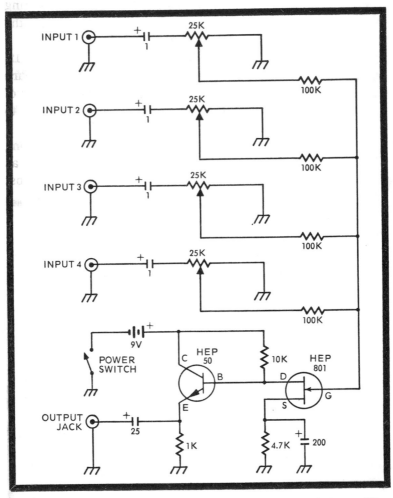

Fig. 3-10. Schematic diagram of four-input audio mixer and preamplifier. A FET is used to excellent advantage here by coupling the high-impedance inputs to the relatively low-impedance emitter-follower amplifier. The result is a high-quality, noise-free output suitable for driving virtually any power amplifier.

pieces. Mount the volume controls along the top outer edge of the upper half, and space them equidistant from each other. Mark the center point for each hole to be melted first, so that you can be sure the holes are lined up just right. Before melting the holes, place a volume control in position where the hole is to be so that you can be absolutely certain the body of the control will fit in the box when the shaft is inserted through the hole. If all elements are okay, go ahead with the melting operation. Mount one control immediately after melting the hole (while the plastic is still warm).

The parts themselves are listed in the table of Fig. 3-12. You will notice that many—indeed most—of the parts are components we have used before. If you've been doing any of the construction projects presented earlier, you'll be likely to have many of these parts on hand already.

Mount the phono jacks on the bottom half of the box, along the back, as pictured in Fig. 3-11. The technique is the same as we've used before, so we won't need to detail it here. The most

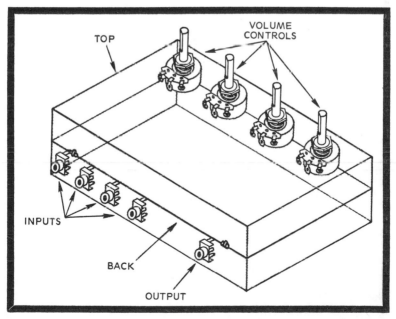

Fig. 3-11. A plastic parts box is used to mount the mixer controls and input-output jacks. A thick box is desirable so that the volume controls won't be allowed to come into contact with the circuit board when the box is closed.

QTY	DESCRIPTION
5	PC-mount phono jacks
4	25K audio taper potentiometers (at least one of which should contain single-pole, single-throw switch)
4	100K ½W carbon composition resistors
1	10K ½W carbon composition resistors
1	4.7K ½W carbon composition resistor
1	1K ½W carbon composition resistor
4	1 uF electrolytic capacitor, PC mounting, 15V
1	25 uF electrolytic capacitor, PC-mounting, 15V
1	200 uF electrolytic capacitor, PC-mounting, 15V
1	npn small-signal transistor, Motorola HEP 50
1	FET, Motorola HEP 801
24	inches shielded wire
18	inches standard hookup wire (22-gage)
25	1499 push-in terminals (Keystone)
1	3 x 4-inch G-pattern prepunched phenolic board
1	9V battery (Eveready 256)
1	9V battery terminal; snap-on, with leads
2	machine screws, with nuts, 2-56 x ¼-inch flathead
1	No. 71 battery holder (Keystone Electronics)

Fig. 3-12. Complete parts list for the four-input audio mixer and preamplifier.

important thing is to have marks prepared first so you can be certain the jacks are lined up nicely and they are not positioned too closely to each other.

After the plastic-box preparation is finished, don't snap the box back together yet. First go ahead with the actual wiring. It is easier for you to run the wires to the jacks if the box is in two separate pieces. And every time you put it together and pull it apart, you're chancing breaking off one of the little hinge snaps.

BOARD WIRING

Since the phono jacks and volume controls are mounted on the box rather than on the board, we insert push-in terminals into the board to use as tie points for these components.

Mount the battery holder first, and secure it with the two 2-56 flathead screws and nuts. Then insert the push-in terminals in the positions shown in Fig. 3-11. Notice that there are 12 push-in terminals along the bottom of the board; these are actually four groups of three, and are the tip points for the volume controls on the plastic box. When these are inserted, place the board in the bottom of the box and set the box cover on loosely to make sure the pins don't come into contact with volume controls. If they do, you'll have to move them back further on the board. If there isn't enough room after rearranging, then you'll simply have to use a larger box. If you buy the parts boxes from one source, you'll find that the bottoms and top are interchangeable. Just buy another box and snap off the thicker of the two halves, then use it in place of one of the two sections of the box you've already prepared.

Once it has been established that the box will accommodate the board with its pins without interfering with the volume controls, you can go ahead with the parts positioning and wiring operations.

Insert all pins as shown first. This will help in your orientation of components. Next, insert the electrolytic capacitors and resistors, bending the leads under the board after each is inserted to hold it in place during wiring and soldering. Watch the capacitor polarities; the positive side of the 25 uF electrolytic points toward the main power pin, while the positive side of the 200 uF electrolytic points in the opposite direction—towards the volume control tie points. The positive leads of the 1 uF devices connect to the pins labeled C in the volume control lineup.

We're only using three pins for the FET, even though the HEP 801 has four leads. The lead we aren't using is the case lead. If you like, you can insert a fourth pin into the board for this lead, then connect a wire from it to the nearest ground-bus point. You have to be careful, though, to make sure the lead doesn't come into contact with any other wires you will be installing.

Once the devices are installed in their positions, but not interconnected or soldered, it's time to wire in the ground bus. The bus is made from a piece of ordinary 20- or 22-gage wire with its insulation stripped off. This lead is soldered to the corner pin marked with a minus sign, then down to the pin marked ground bus (A). Similar lengths of the wire connect all the A terminals in the front lower section of the board.

The balance of the wiring is all quite straightforward, and you can easily accomplish it by checking the layout of Fig. 3-13 as you work. It doesn't make any difference where leads tie to the ground bus, so if it is inconvenient to tie any of the leads to the points shown, let them terminate at the nearest likely place along the ground-bus line.

The 100K resistors tie together on one end, as shown. To avoid the necessity of using additional wire, let the component leads themselves be used for the interconnects. This is easy to do if you start with the resistor on the far right, bringing its lead all the way over to the next resistor before you make the joint. If you use the same procedure for each of the four resistors, by the time you get to the resistor on the extreme left, you can use its lead to connect directly to the gate terminal (G) where the FET will be connected.

After the board is fully wired (including the standard checking and double-checking), you can do the interconnecting between the circuit board and the box-mounted components.

Shielded wire must be used for the input circuits. High-impedance circuits must be shielded to prevent the pickup of

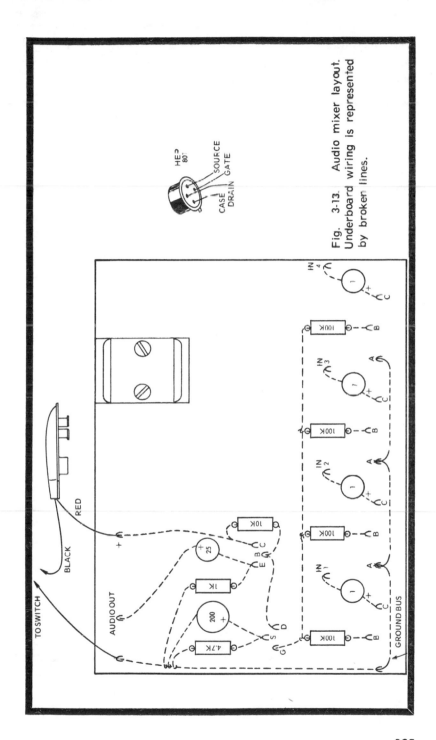

Fig. 3-13. Audio mixer layout. Underboard wiring is represented by broken lines.

105

radiation and stray fields, which is interpreted in the output as hum. Determine the lengths of shielded lead you'll need (you need four pieces, each connected between an input jack and the associated "in" terminal on the board). Cut the pieces about an inch longer than you need.

Prepare the shielded lead by cutting the insulation back about an inch from each end of each piece. Then, use a small screwdriver to separate the wires in the shielded outer wire adjacent to the insulation, as shown in Fig. 3-14. Pull the inner

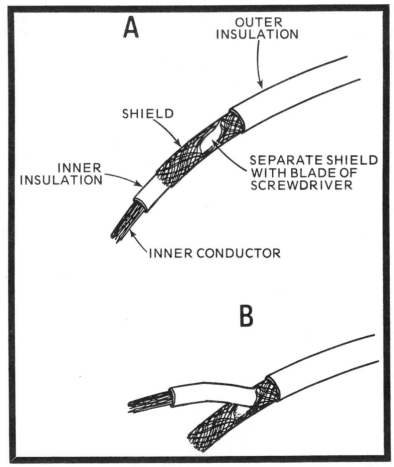

Fig. 3-14. Prepare the shielded lead by stripping back the outer insulation. Use a small screwdriver to separate the shield strands near the insulation (A), then pull the inner conductor out through the separated section, as shown in B.

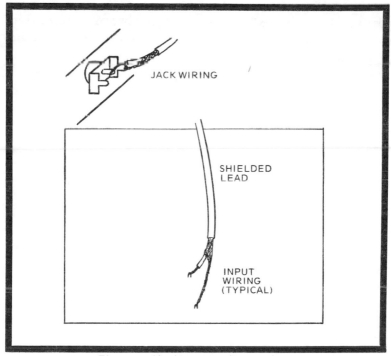

Fig. 3-15. Shielded-lead terminations.

conductor up through the shield at the separation. When all the ends have been prepared as shown, they may be attached to the phono jacks mounted on the box . Don't connect the board ends until after the shielded leads have all been terminated at the jacks; this will simplify the last remaining soldering operations.

Figure 3-15 shows how the shielded leads are soldered to the jacks and board terminals. At each jack, the shield connects to one of the jack mounting ears, and the inner conductor is soldered to the center pin. On the board, each wire terminates in its numbered "in" terminal pair. The inner conductor will solder to the pin marked "in" and the outer conductor (shield) will connect to the assocaited ground-bus marked with the A designator. Be sure that none of the fine wire threads from the shield touch any of the other terminals. If the ground bus or shield makes contact with any of the inner-conductor connections, the mixer won't get audio from that input.

All that remains to be done now is the wiring of the volume controls. The fact that the volume controls are positioned in close proximity to the pins where they will be connected means that shielded wire needs to be used here. Use individual wires of the shortest lengths you can, and solder the terminals as pictured in Fig. 3-16. Be careful not to reverse the two outer leads on the controls' three-terminal groups; otherwise, the volume controls will work backwards. And if the power switch is part of one of the controls, it will make turn-on quite cumbersome, since the volume for that input will be at maximum as soon as the switch clicks on.

There is no real requirement for the switch to be on any of the controls; it could be any single-pole toggle or slide switch. But an additional switch does create positioning and mounting difficulties, so it seems more practical to incorporate the switch into one of the controls. If all controls are equipped with such switches, use the switch on the extreme left control, just to stay conventional.

While wiring of the switch is not actually shown because of the multiplicity of possible approaches, the basic routing is pictured in Fig. 3-13. All you have to do is cut the black battery wire and run the two cut pieces to the switch. Since the switch is a simple make-and-break arrangement, there is no polarity problem to be concerned with.

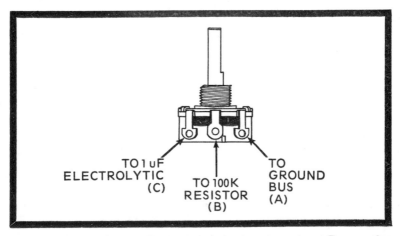

Fig. 3-16. Each volume control is to be wired as shown here. Transposing the outer terminal leads will make the control work in reverse.

Project 9

Proximity Detector and Touch Switch

Whether you just want to turn a light on or off or set up a
sophisticated burglar alarm, the touch switch circuit shown in
Fig. 3-17 will prove fun to build and educational as well. One of
the most effective features of this device is its simplicity; you
can put one together easily in no more than a couple of hours,
once you have the parts all together.

APPLICATIONS

Depending on the length of wire you use for the sensor and
the setting of the 25M potentiometer, the touch switch (officially, a capacitance-triggered automatic relay) can be used
to detect body proximity or body touch. In the most sensitive
position, when a human body gets close to the sensor lead, the
relay portion of the switch will close, applying 115V household
power to the convenience receptacle mounted on the plastic
parts box. Whatever you have plugged into the outlet will turn
on (a lamp, a bell, etc.). When the body moves away, the power
will be removed from the outlet. In the less sensitive mode, a
lamp will come on when the sensor is actually touched, and it
will go off when the hand is moved.

To use the unit as a burglar alarm, simply connect the
sensor wire to a doorknob or other metal piece that can be
used as a trigger. An unauthorized person will set off the
alarm when he touches the trigger piece.

I haven't employed the touch switch as a burglar alarm,
but I have an application that serves me quite well: I have the
sensor lead connected to the metal back of my desk chair, and
have my incandescent desk lamp plugged into the box. When I
sit down at the desk, my body capacitance causes the FET to

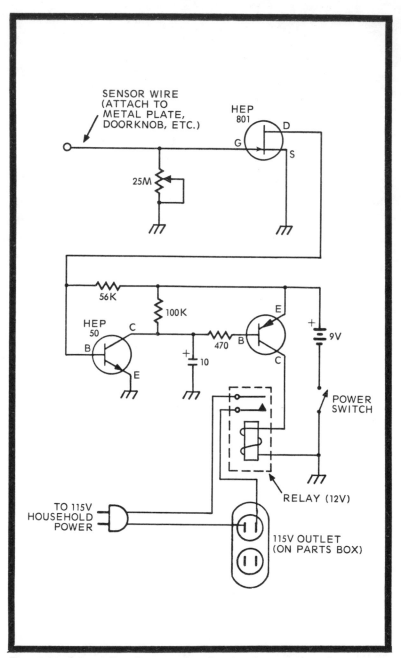

Fig. 3-17. Schematic diagram for the touch switch and proximity detector. The outlet and power switch should be mounted on top of the plastic parts box.

draw current, which drives the transistor controlling the relay. In short, when I sit, my desk lamp comes on; when I get up, it turns off.

You will doubtless be able to think of a myriad other useful applications for the device. If it serves no other purpose, it certainly is a unique conversation piece. It always takes a considerable amount of time before my guests figure out what makes my desk lamp go on and off automatically.

PRECAUTIONS

The touch switch is sensitive to stray fields because the input impedance is so high. As a matter of fact, the extremely high input impedance of the device is the reason it works in the first place. But this fact makes the unit particularly suscep- tible to fields caused by adjacent transformers, motors, and power lines. Thus, the sensor wire cannot be connected to any metal household appliance such as the refrigerator, electric stove, radio, or electric typewriter.

Also, if the sensor wire is unduly long, it will be triggered into the constant on state by the inherent capacitance of the wire itself. The body capacitance of an intruder will be negligible by comparison, so it will go undetected. Your best bet is to determine the maximum length by the empirical method (trial-and-error) until you reach a maximum. Then make it a point to keep the sensor wire shorter than that maximum. The maximum may be exceeded, but you'll have to use shielded wire for all but the portion that serves as the trigger. And the outer conductor of the wire will have to be grounded at both ends.

The parts are listed in Fig. 3-18. The only "new" elements we use are a pnp transistor and the relay. Any conventional 12V dc relay will be satisfactory, so long as the contacts can handle the amount of current required by your 115V load. (A 100W lamp will draw slightly more than 1A; so if your relay is the standard 2A contact variety, you'll have to keep the lamp to no more than about 100W maximum.)

LAYOUT AND CONSTRUCTION

The layout you use will depend to a large extent on the relay you employ. I was fortunate enough to find a relay that is

QTY	DESCRIPTION
1	HEP 50 npn transistor (Motorola)
1	HEP 51 pnp transistor (Motorola)
1	HEP 801 FET (Motorola)
1	12V dc relay
1	10uF, 15V electrolytic capacitor
1	470-ohm, ½W carbon composition resistor
1	47K ½W carbon composition resistor
1	100K ½W carbon composition resistor
1	25M PC-mount trimmer potentiometer
1	push-in terminals
1	9V battery holder (No. 71, Keystone Electronics)
1	9V battery terminal (snap-on, with leads)
24	inches hookup wire
1	3 x 4-inch G-pattern prepunched phenolic board
2	2-56 x ¼-inch machine screws with nuts
1	single-pole, single-throw switch

Fig. 3-18. Proximity detector and touch switch parts list.

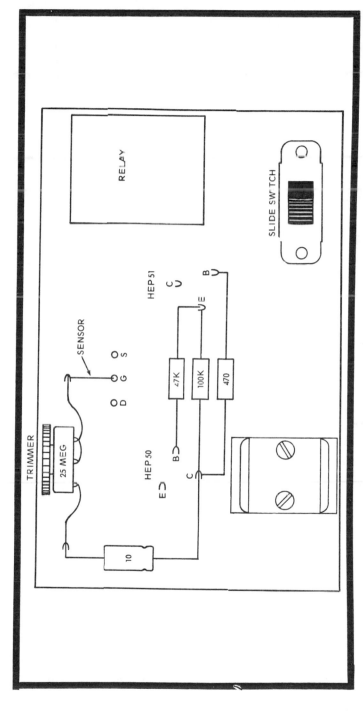

Fig. 3-19. Layout of the proximity detector and touch switch. If the unit is to be box-mounted, the sensor-wire contact should be melted into the box surface.

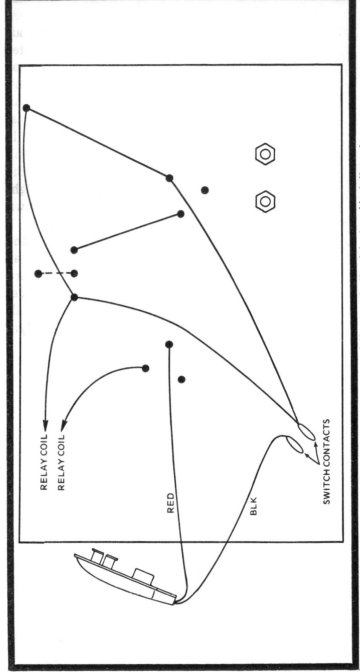

RELAY COIL

RELAY COIL

RED

BLK

SWITCH CONTACTS

Fig. 3-20. Underboard wiring of the proximity detector. Variations in relay pin-connection arrangements may affect the placement of components to some extent.

not much larger than a couple of postage stamps. It has contacts that plug directly into the holes of the G-pattern board. Since the relay I used was a military surplus unit, your chances of duplicating it are slim. The next best bet is a Potter & Brumfield RS5-D (12V coil). This relay doesn't take too much space and it is fairly inexpensive. Since the holes don't match perfectly with those of the board, you'll have to ream out a few of the existing holes to accommodate the relay pins.

Figure 3-19 shows the basic layout I used, which is adaptable if you use the RS5-D. The only major difference will be in the pin layout for the relay itself. Since the pins for the relay represent the only aspect of the touch switch that might be construed as "complex," the underboard wiring is shown also (Fig. 3-20).

Install the relay and battery holder first. Then insert the push-in terminals as close to the positions shown in Fig. 3-19 as possible. If you can wire in all the basic components before soldering, the end result will be much neater in appearance. After all wires and leads are properly terminated, solder all the joints. Finally, solder in the FET, the npn and the pnp transistors.

Project 10
Moisture Detector

Up till now the projects have been presented pictorially, schematically, and in considerable depth. The idea of the detail was to help you get acquainted with basic semiconductors. As you build projects, however, you gain experience, and with experience comes self-confidence. This project—a moisture detector—and the two subsequent projects involve the same semiconductors used in the proximity detector: the HEP 801 FET, the HEP 50 npn bipolar transistor, and the pnp bipolar transistor. Each of the projects also is made to work with the same relay used for the proximity detector. The chief differences are in the passive components used and in the basic circuit configuration.

You'll see no pictorials for this project or any of the subsequent projects. Part of the fun of building is in the laying out of the components on the board. You can use the same basic philosophy, of course—perfboard, battery holder, enclosure in a plastic parts box—but the layout is strictly up to your own imagination. We give you the circuit diagrams and parts lists. We even offer special pointers where they're warranted. But the rest is up to you.

The moisture detector is triggered by water bridging a gridwork of wires. You can make the gridwork by stringing bare wire over a piece of G-pattern board as shown in Fig. 3-21. The gridwork is wired into the basic alarm circuit as shown in the schematic diagram of Fig. 3-22. Parts are listed in Fig. 3-23.

The basic layout of the moisture detector can be quite similar to that of the proximity detector, since the actual component count is similar and the semiconductor lineup is the same. As with the previous projects, this unit will fit easily into a standard parts box. The gridwork, of course, should be mounted some distance away.

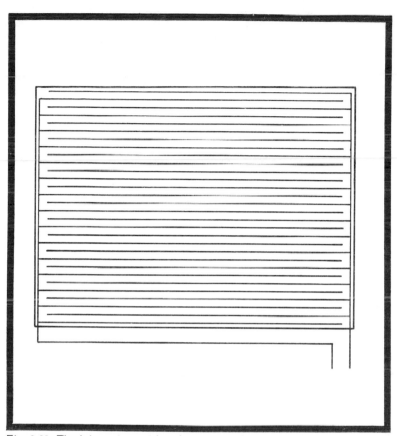

Fig. 3-21. The triggering gridwork consists of bare wire strung over a G-pattern perfboard. When moisture bridges any pair of adjacent wires, the relay will pull in, sounding an alarm or turning on a light. A finger touch on the grid will also activate the alarm.

Since the gridwork serves as a high-value resistor, any type of conductive contact that joins the grid wires will cause the relay to trigger. This means that you can use the grid as a touch point to turn lamps on and off. Another worthwhile application is as a burglar alarm. You can probably think of a wide variety of ways to deploy the device in this service, either as a normally closed relay, that keeps a light on until something metal is removed from the gridwork, or as a normally open relay, which turns on a light or alarm when any of the wires are bridged. You'll find the basic relay circuit quite useful. The projects to follow demonstrate that fact quite well.

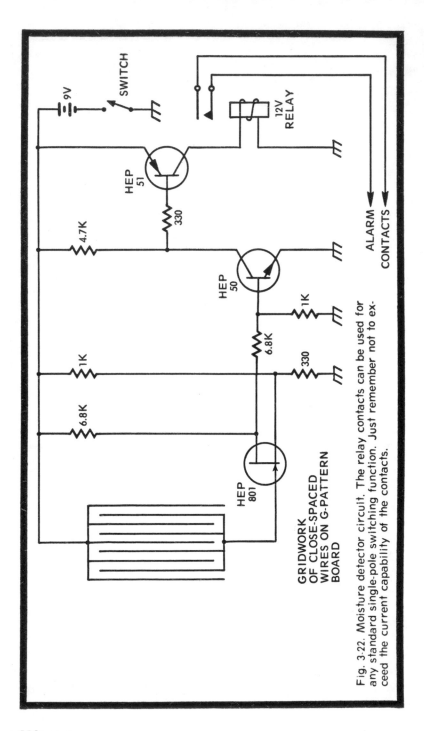

Fig. 3-22. Moisture detector circuit. The relay contacts can be used for any standard single-pole switching function. Just remember not to exceed the current capability of the contacts.

QTY	DESCRIPTION
2	G-pattern perfboards (one 3 x 4-inch for circuit board use, one any size for stringing the grid wires).
1	long section bare wire, 22-gage, solid.
*	No. 1499 push-in terminal, snap-on, with leads
1	9V battery terminal, snap-on, with leads
1	9V battery holder (Keystone Electronics No. 71)
1	9V battery (Eveready 256 or equivalent)
2	machine screws, with nuts
1	12V dc relay (Potter & Brumfield RS5-D)
1	SPST switch (any type)
7	½W carbon composition resistors:
	2 6.8K
	2 1K
	2 330
	1 4.7K
1	HEP 801 FET (Motorola)
1	HEP 50 npn bipolar transistor (Motorola)
1	HEP 51 pnp bipolar transistor (Motorola)

*Use as many as required. Previous projects will serve as a guide.

Fig. 3-23. Moisture detector parts list.

Project 11
Light-Activated Relay

Light-operated devices are among the most useful crime deterrents these days. Properly connected, they allow house lights to come on automatically at night, even when the homeowners are many miles away. They "tattle" when any light comes on in places where it shouldn't. There's almost no limit to the burglar-alarm possibilities of light devices. But their capabilities range even further.

If the contacts of the relay section are husky enough to withstand the high-current drain, a light-operated relay can be used to turn on the coffee maker each morning at dawn, for example. And such a device mounted in a dark garage can be used to turn on the garage light whenever the beam from a pair of headlamps strikes the photocell surface.

In a small office, the light-operated relay can be used for a multitude of purposes. It can remove power from office machines at night, for example, and apply power automatically and simultaneously to regular outdoor or night lights. The utility of the relay is limited only by the imagination of the user.

Figure 3-24 shows the basic circuit. It should look familiar to you, because it bears a striking similarity to the moisture detector of Project 10. The only difference is the triggering circuit, which includes a photocell and a 1M potentiometer.

You can use the parts list presented in Project 10. Just add the two items. The photocell is available from Meshna Surplus, East Lynn, Massachusetts ($1 each). The potentiometer should be a linear-taper, carbon film type, designed for circuit board mounting. You will have no trouble finding this control at your local electronics dealer.

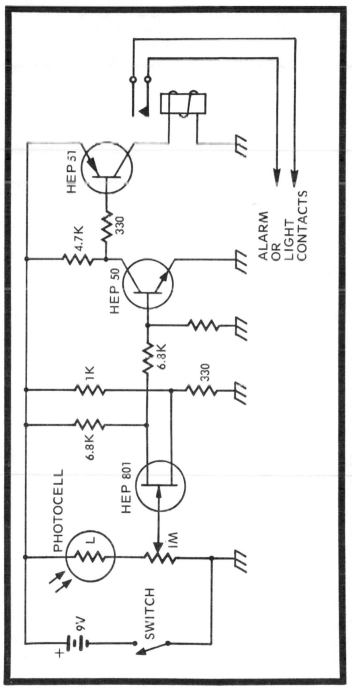

Fig. 3-24. Light-operated relay schematic. Notice the similarity between this project and the moisture detector. The difference is the FET triggering scheme.

121

The control adjusts the sensitivity of the relay, and it is necessary to keep the relay from triggering with light beams that are not meant to cause triggering. The relay you use will depend on the application. If you plan to use the light-operated relay in a more or less conventional manner (turning on a switch to a low-power load when sufficient light falls on the surface of the photocell), you will only need a standard single-pole device such as the Potter & Brumfield RS5-D. However, if you want to retain a maximum of functional switching capability—perhaps controlling one circuit in darkness and one in daylight—you'll need a heavy-duty relay of the single-pole, double-throw variety, as shown in Fig. 3-25.

In this latter application, two independently wired outlets are wired from the relay so that during daylight hours one circuit is activated and during darkness the other is. The two 115V circuits are never alive at the same time, due to the wiring scheme at the relay contacts.

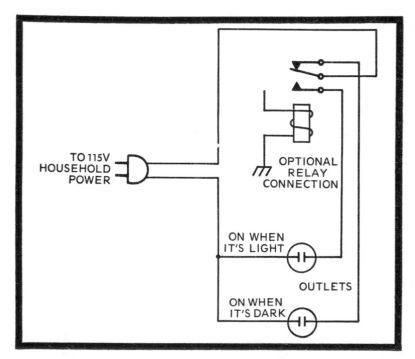

Fig. 3-25. If a single-pole, double-throw relay is substituted for the RS5-D, the capability of the device is multiplied.

Project 12
Adjustable Timer

Demonstrating the versatility of the "alarm" circuit we've been using in the past few projects is the variable timer, the schematic of which is presented in Fig. 3-26. As you can see, the basics are the same; as a matter of fact, the parts list for the moisture detector will take care of all the parts for the timer with only these additional components: a 100K ½W resistor, a 100 uF electrolytic capacitor, and a 5M PC-mounting linear-taper trimmer potentiometer. There is nothing critical about the add-on components, either. You can use a larger electrolytic capacitor (which results in more time), or a lower value trimmer potentiometer (which results in less time and a reduced time spread).

If you examine the circuit, you will see that the philosophy of operation is the same as for the previous circuits. The input is the only different element. In this case, the FET gets its input signal when the power switch is turned on. The switch closes the power circuit, which allows battery voltage to be fed to the timer. The electrolytic keeps the FET in the off state until it reaches a certain point in its state of charge, at which time the voltage on the positive side of the capacitor is high enough to allow the FET to start conducting. When the FET conducts, the relay pulls in.

The time is governed by the setting of the 5M trimmer. If you use the values shown, you will have a time spread of 5 seconds to about 50 seconds. The higher the value of the potentiometer, the longer it will take the capacitor to charge and the longer it will take the relay to pull in.

This circuit is particularly useful in the darkroom, where it can be used to key a bell or buzzer to signify completion of development. If the single-pole, double-throw relay hookup

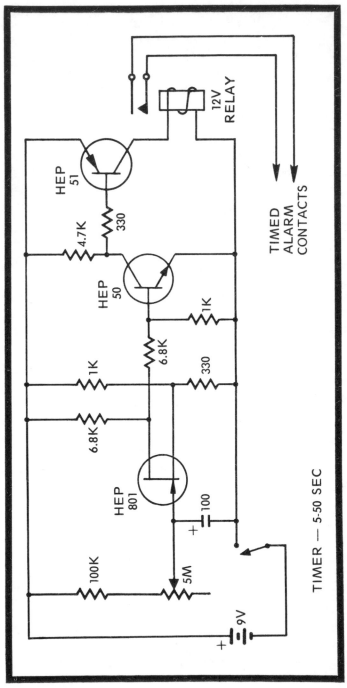

TIMER — 5-50 SEC

Fig. 3-26. Adjustable timer schematic. The relay is energized after the power is applied. The length of time varies (from 5 to 50 seconds), depending on the setting of the 5M trimmer potentiometer.

124

shown in Fig. 3-25 is used with the timer, it can be extremely useful as a garage-light control. In this application, the lights can be made to stay on until the termination of the timed period, thereby allowing you to get safely into the house before the garage goes dark.

Project 13
Alarm Warbler

Many of the projects presented in this book are applicable for use as burglar alarms. But a burglar alarm is hardly effective unless something noteworthy happens when it is actuated. At night, of course, lights are often effective . . . but not always. And lights are totally useless as burglar-chasers during daylight hours.

Oscillators are good noisemakers as a rule, but in a noisy environment the monotonous wail of an oscillator might easily go unnoticed. An alternative is an oscillator with a pitch that varies continuously and automatically during operation. The schematic of Fig. 3-27 shows a simple and easy-to-build oscillator that should serve very well in burglar alarm applications. It uses a pair of HEP 310 unijunctions to create its low-level varying tone.

Since the oscillator circuit shown in Fig. 3-27 contains no amplifier, it will have to be used in conjunction with one. If you built up the FET and bipolar amplifier circuit of Project 7, you'll find it to be the perfect complement for this warbler. To retain a maximum of versatility, however, it is best to keep the two units separated on two circuit boards.

The warbler will fit easily onto a 2 x 3 inch phenolic board. Enclose it in a plastic box, and interconnect it with the amplifier using shielded lead as shown.

Figure 3-28 lists the parts.

COMBINING AN AMPLIFIER

Where extremely high power is not a prime requirement, such as alarm applications involving comparatively small places, you can include an efficient one-transistor amplifier right on the board with the warbler. In this case, however, you

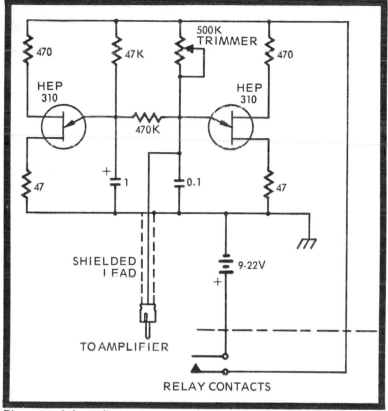

Fig. 3-27. Schematic diagram of the basic dual-unijunction warbler alarm. The output should be fed into a high powered amplifier.

should use a larger board. The layout diagram of Fig. 3-29 shows how the two circuits are integrated on a single board. The higher the battery voltages, incidentally, the louder your warbler will be. The semiconductors will handle up to 24V dc without damage; but few are the places where power sources of that voltage are found. The amplifier-warbler combination should operate extremely well from an auto battery, though, which makes this circuit an ideal candidate for car theft-alarm applications.

Figure 3-30 shows the overall warbler-amplifier circuit; you will notice that it differs little from the basic circuit of Fig. 3-27. The chief difference is that the signal from the warbler is derived from the second unijunction's base 1 terminal.

To obtain as much loudness as possible, it is important to get the best attainable impedance match between the speaker and the amplifier stage. To accomplish this objective, we use a small audio transformer with a primary impedance of 1000 ohms and a secondary impedance to match the speaker itself. Transformers with 8-ohm secondaries are quite commonly available and inexpensive, so that's probably the best choice.

The trimmer control adjusts the pitch of the warbler. If you adjust the trimmer with the unit on, you will notice one

QTY	DESCRIPTION
2	47-ohm ½W carbon composition resistors
2	470-ohm ½W carbon composition resistors
1	470K ½W carbon composition resistor
1	47K ½W carbon composition resistor
2	HEP 310 unijunction transistors (Motorola)
1	1 uF electrolytic capacitor, 15V
1	0.1 uF disc ceramic capacitor, 15V
1	short length shielded lead, with RCA-plug termination
*	push-in terminals (Keystone No. 1499)
1	2 x 3-inch phenolic perfboard (G pattern)
1	9V battery (Eveready 256 or equivalent)
1	9V battery terminal; snap-on, with leads
1	9V battery holder (Keystone Electronics No. 71)
2	2-56 machine screws, with nuts
1	500K PC-mount trimmer potentiometer

* Use as many as required

Fig. 3-28. Warbler alarm parts list.

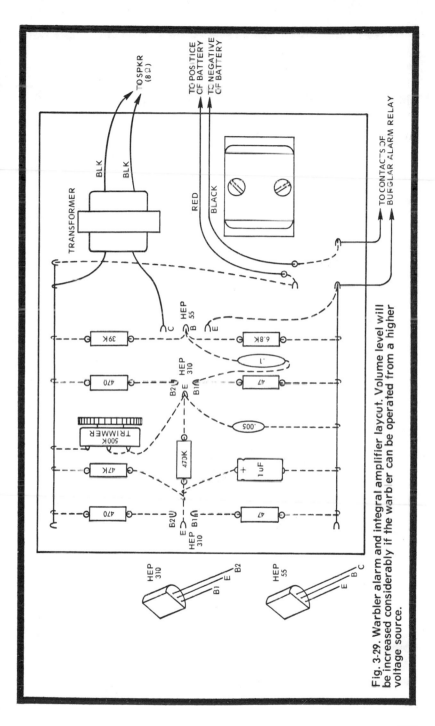

Fig. 3-29. Warbler alarm and integral amplifier layout. Volume level will be increased considerably if the warbler can be operated from a higher voltage source.

129

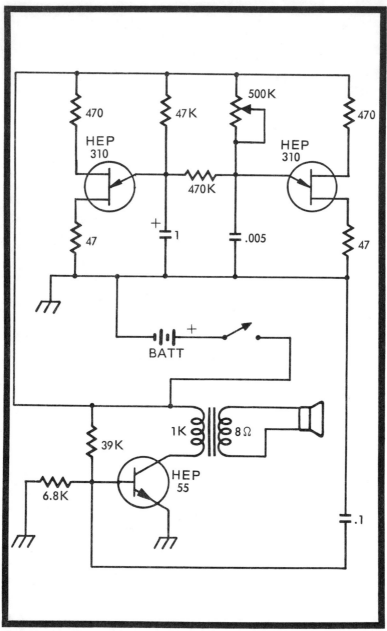

Fig. 3-30. Warbler-amplifier combination. With 16-18V dc, the output is extremely loud and piercing. The warble rate is set by 1 uF capacitor. A larger value will slow the warble rate. The pitch of the varying wail is adjusted with the 500K trimmer potentiometer.

QTY	DESCRIPTION
2	47-ohm ½W carbon composition resistors
2	470-ohm ½W carbon composition resistors
1	47K ½W carbon composition resistor
1	6.8K ½W carbon composition resistor
1	39K ½W carbon composition resistor
1	470K ½W carbon composition resistor
1	500K PC-mount trimmer potentiometer
1	1 uF electrolytic capacitor
1	0.1 uF disc ceramic capacitor
1	0.005 uF disc ceramic capacitor
1	audio transformer (miniature), 1000 ohms primary, 8 ohms secondary
2	HEP 310 unijunction transistors (Motorola)
1	HEP 55 npn power transistor (Motorola)
15	push-in terminal pins (Keystone No. 1499)
1	3 x 4-inch G-pattern prepunched phenolic board
1	miniature 8-ohm speaker
1	battery holder (if unit is to be operated from a transistor radio battery)
2	2-56 machine screws with nuts (if a battery holder is used)
1	9V battery terminal; snap-on, with leads (if battery is to be used)
1	battery (9-24V)

Fig. 3-31. Warbler amplifier parts list.

spot where the audio is almost too piercing to listen to. The level will seem to drop slightly when the control is increased, even though the pitch will be higher. Lower settings of the control give a buzz-like sound.

The repetition rate of the warbler is set by the value of the electrolytic capacitor on the first unijunction's emitter terminal. The 1 uF capacitor gives a very rapid warble that makes the alarm sound like something out of a science-fiction movie. Higher values of capacitance give progressively slower wails. Most published circuits show a 10 uF electrolytic here, but I think the 1 uF device results in a sound that is a great deal more attention-getting.

Practicing With Principles

In the preceding section you had the opportunity to try your hand at circuit layout. From the results, you should know whether you have a natural knack for it or not. In the latter event, perhaps a few hints will be worthwhile for you to learn. No matter how many components are required in any given project, no matter how complex the project, you should have some idea as to what the physical appearance of the device you're building will be when you're finished.

Sound tough? It really is, particularly for the newly initiated electronics experimenter. But with a little practice, the task gets simpler. Of course, the fewer the components your circuit will require, the easier it will be to form a mental image of what the unit will look like when you're finished. That is why it will be felicitous for you to begin in layout design by employing simple circuits. As you get confidence in your ability, you can graduate to more sophisticated projects.

One of the absolute necessities is for you to recognize each component printed on the schematic diagram. By this time, you are already familiar with a fairly large number of components, and you can readily recognize them when you see them presented schematically. There are a host of other devices, though, that are common enough in practice but that you haven't yet worked with. These include transformers (although the final project of the preceding section did incorporate one), coils, relays, a variety of solid-state devices, and some miscellaneous electronic "hybrids."

You won't be working with many different types of components to build the projects in this book, but you should spend a little time getting acquainted with new devices; you'll be interested in buying other books and building other projects, and it will save you a lot of time and effort if you have learned to recognize the schematic symbols and what they represent.

TRANSFORMERS

A transformer does one job: it converts an alternating voltage to either a higher or lower voltage value. It can be as small as a pea or as large as a house. In general, however, your experimenting will be done with transformers ranging in size from about one cubic inch to units of about 30 cubic inches. The key parameters of transformers are power-handling capability, impedance ratio, and frequency of input voltage. Nonetheless, there are myriads of transformers listed in catalogs according to their category of usage. The two you'll use the most in transistor experiments are audio and power types Figure 4-1 shows the schematic symbol for a transformer as well as sketches of several case styles.

Audio Transformers

An audio transformer is designed to accept an ac signal within the audible spectrum and change it to a level suitable for processing by the next stage in an electronic circuit. If the transformer is used to couple an audio stage to a speaker, it is called an **output transformer**. If it is used to couple a transducer (microphone, for example) to an initial audio stage, it is called an **input transformer**. Transformers used to couple a signal from one stage to another within a circuit are called **interstage transformers**. Complicating things still further, if any of the above transformers happen to be small and particularly suited to solid-state circuits, they are often referred to in the catalogs as **transistor transformers**.

As it happens, an output transformer can be used as an input transformer as often as not. All you have to do is use the primary winding for the secondary and vice versa.

Audio transformers have a characteristic primary and secondary impedance. The impedance gives you a clue to the ultimate use of the transformer in a circuit. If you see a schematic that calls for a transformer with a primary impedance of 1000 ohms and a secondary impedance of 3, 2, 4, or 8 ohms, you will know the transformer is an output type. The primary impedance of 1000 ohms tells you the transformer is a good match for the output stage of a common-emitter transistor amplifier. The low secondary impedance tells you the transformer will mate well to a speaker. A transformer with a primary impedance of 10,000 ohms and a secondary impedance of 2000 ohms will likely be an interstage transformer.

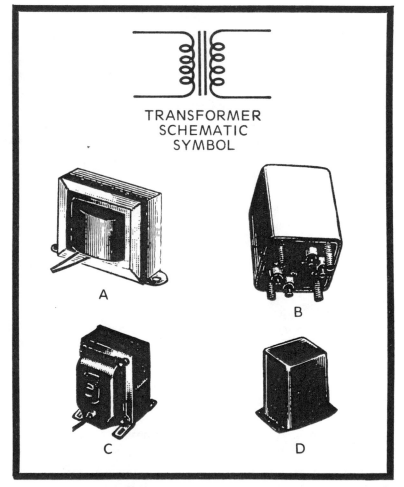

Fig. 4-1. Several transformer case styles are shown here with the universally accepted schematic symbol. Style A is usually reserved for low-power applications (audio or power); style B is a "military-type" high-voltage power transformer; styles C and D are for medium-power applications.

Power Transformers

A power transformer is used to change the alternating line voltage at your home to a level suitable for powering any electronic circuit you might be building. In practice, however, the term "power" has come to mean high voltage; this means that most catalogs that list power transformers will show secondary voltages of at least 125V for one winding. (Many have additional windings with lower voltages on them.)

Power transformers, like audio transformers, are classed according to function. There are plate transformers, filament transformers, control transformers, and isolation transformers.

Plate Transformer. A plate transformer is used to change household line voltage to a voltage suitable for rectifying and supplying the anodes of a vacuum-tube circuit. The anode of a tube is frequently referred to as a plate, hence the name.

Filament Transformer. A transformer used exclusively for supplying the filament voltage for vacuum tubes is referred to as a filament transformer. Though most filament transformer secondaries are 6.3 or 12.6V, there are other secondary voltages available.

Control Transformers. These transformers get the name from the application they initially had almost exclusively: controlling electronic circuits. The output from a control transformer, typically 6, 16, or 24V, is rectified and used to power the relays and other control devices in a circuit. Transistor circuits use control transformers because they are ideal from an output voltage standpoint. A control transformer typically has the shape of the unit pictured in Fig. 4-1A.

Isolation Transformer. As the name implies, the chief application of this transformer is isolation. Isolation transformers typically offer little, if any, step-up or -down capability. They are used for safety, to avoid the necessity of allowing a chassis to be part of the electrical circuit in which they are used.

In most electronic circuits, the chassis is used as a common grounding point, and all voltage lines are referenced to it. This is extremely safe if the electrical cord is always plugged into the wall so the chassis ground is always plugged into the wall properly. One side of your two-prong wall plug connects directly to a waterpipe or other earth ground system; the other side carries lethal voltage. When the chassis itself connects to the side of the prong that connects to the earth ground, there is practically no possibility of getting an electrical shock when you touch it. However, if the plug is reversed, the chassis becomes "hot"—connected to the voltage side of the line. You could get killed!

The isolation transformer obviates that contingency by allowing the household power to be inductively coupled into the electrical circuit. That way, both sides of the circuit's input voltage line are isolated from the household wiring.

Learning to Determine Size

The physical size of a transformer can be estimated if you know what the unit will be used for. That way, you can look a schematic over without even buying the parts and know how much space it will take up. It will help, for example, in determining the chassis size requirements.

Look at the schematic of Fig. 4-2. Can you tell by looking at the diagram how much physical volume would be required to enclose the unit completely? Do you know how you would mount the transformer?

The clue is power. The transformer specified in the diagram has a primary voltage requirement of 115V (60 Hz), and its secondary winding provides 6.3V at 1A. The total power-handling capacity of about 6½W (voltage multiplied by current yields wattage, or power) tells you the transformer is likely to be quite small—small enough, in fact, to fit onto one of our 3 x 4 inch phenolic perfboards. (If you order part 33 P 37029 from Lafayette, 111 Jericho Turnpike, Syosset, Long Island, New York 11791, you will find the transformer has two mounting holes spaced 2¼ inches center-to-center. The transformer sells for $1.39.)

Audio transformers can be judged the same way—by power. For transistor use, power is seldom specified in the description of an audio transformer. When there is no specific power requirement, you can assume the power is an insignificant parameter, and the size of the transformer will be no more than a couple of cubic inches.

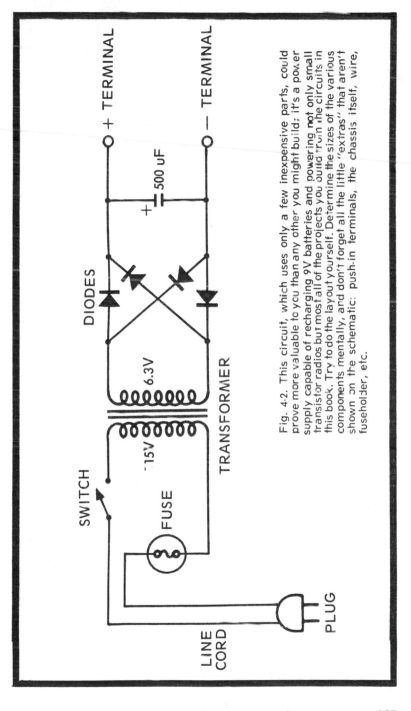

Fig. 4-2. This circuit, which uses only a few inexpensive parts, could prove more valuable to you than any other you might build; it's a power supply capable of recharging 9V batteries and powering not only small transistor radios but most all of the projects you build in the circuits in this book. Try to do the layout yourself. Determine the sizes of the various components mentally, and don't forget all the little "extras" that aren't shown on the schematic: push-in terminals, the chassis itself, wire, fuseholder, etc.

Another way to judge transformer size is according to its frequency of operation. The higher in frequency a transformer is designed to work, the fewer the number of laminations required in its core. The lower in frequency, the heavier the core. Ordinary audio transformers are designed to work in the range above 75 or 100 Hz, which allows relatively small core sizes. Hi-fi transformers, however, which are required to faithfully pass signals below 50 Hz, often require cores that are quite thick.

Probably the most important single characteristic of a transformer is the fact that you can't get direct current to pass through it, at least not for more than one tiny instant. If you connect the primary wires of a transformer to a dc source, you'll get a brief surge of the proper secondary voltage, and then the output will disappear until you either reverse the polarity of the applied dc signal or you shut off the dc source altogether; either choice will result in another quick secondary-voltage surge.

RELAYS

A relay (Fig. 4-3) is an electromechanical switch. It is so complicated—with its armature, coil, contacts, mounting problems, and power requirements—that most people who first learn the function of the device wonder why an ordinary manual switch isn't used in place of it. After all, it usually takes a manual switch to supply the voltage to operate the relay in the first place.

When you look at the reasons why relays are used, you'll realize why they are an indispensiable part of electronics. The horn and the starter on your automobile are both relay-operated. If it were economically feasible to dispense with the relays, and let the horn button supply power directly to the horn and the ignition switch supply power directly to the starter, you can be sure that's the way it would be done. Unfortunately, both the horn and the starter (and the headlights, and a number of other normal automotive functions) draw a very large amount of current. A starter, for example, which has to create enough energy to turn a cold engine over after a freezing night, might draw as much as 100A or more. If the ignition switch were built to handle that kind of power, it would take up a tremendous amount of under-dash space. And the

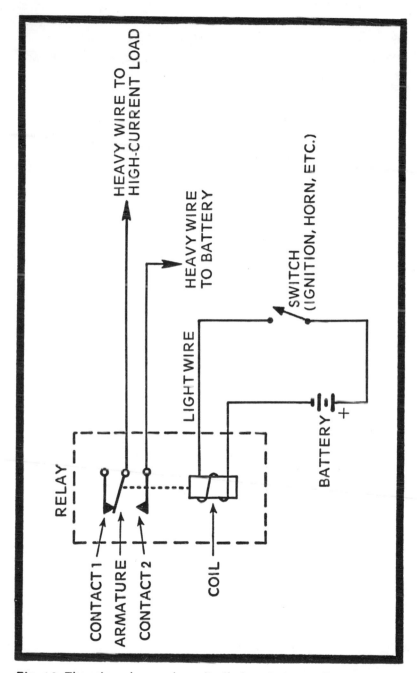

Fig. 4-3. The relay, shown schematically here in broken lines, Is an in-
dispensable part of your car's electrical system.

wires required to handle 100A loads without significant losses over the distance from the battery to the ignition switch and back to the starter would have to have huge diameters— possibly more than ½ inch. Connecting wires of that size to a switch isn't easy either, as one look at the terminals of your battery will attest. The longer the wire, the heavier the current losses on long runs.

The answer is, of course, the relay. The relay is installed between the battery and the starter. Another relay is installed between the battery and the headlights, and between the battery and the horn. This way, the heavy wires aren't quite so heavy because the runs are relatively short. You can't however, crawl under the hood and perform the necessary switching operations of your car when switching is called for. So you activate the relays electrically.

Relay coils require very little power, generally. In most cases they require but a tiny fraction of the power they actually switch. A relay that controls 100A of current can operate with less than 1A of drain. Thus, the horn button is wired with a light-gage electrical wire that is used to supply operating voltage to the horn relay; the relay does the power switching. Light wiring under the dash allows a starter relay to be energized with little power drain, even though 100A or more passes through the relay contacts on the way to the starter.

Power switching is only one function of relays; there are many. The telephone company, for example, has used relays for many years in timing applications. With a single energization pulse to a relay coil, several circuits may be connected, others disconnected. Variations in coils allow some circuits to be switched rapidly, others slowly; one relay can disconnect some circuits before connecting others, or cause several circuit connections before disconnecting any of those already connected.

A relay is a powerful electromagnet; it consists of a coil of wire wrapped around a metal core. When a dc voltage is supplied to the coil, the metal core becomes suddenly magnetized and attracts the metal armature (Fig. 4-3). The armature is mechanically attached to a pointer that serves as the movable pole piece of a conventional switch. You can see what happen to the relay contacts in Fig. 4-3 if the armature is pulled toward the coil suddenly: The armature breaks the circuit at contact 1 and makes a circuit at contact 2.

In practice, relays are sized according to (1) the number of circuits they are required to make or break, and (2) the amount of current the contacts are required to switch. For most electronic applications, current requirements are in the milliamperes (though there are numerous exceptions), and there are rarely more than two poles.

OTHER PASSIVE DEVICES

Look at the schematic symbols presented in Fig. 4-4 and see how many of them you recognize. These are all very common components in electronics, and it would be difficult to build more than but a few circuit projects without running into nearly all of them. If you've been building the projects in this book, you have already had the chance to work with the resistor (A), the potentiometer (B), the capacitor (D and E), the electrolytic capacitor (I), the switch (P), battery (R), the momentary-contact switch (U), the chassis ground (X), and the tie point (Y). You may recognize some of the others, but there are probably a few that you haven't seen before.

C, for example, is a photoresistive cell. The device looks very much like the symbol—a circular field on which is imprinted a zigzag line of photoconductive material, such as cadmium sulfide. The cell is a high-value resistor when it's dark. When light strikes the imprinted surface, however, the device's resistance decreases enormously, sometimes to a mere fraction of the device's dark resistance. The cell can be used in series with a relay coil wire, for example, to keep the relay from being energized until enough light strikes the surface to overcome the resistance.

The two arrows adjacent to the photoresistive cell tell you that the device is light-operated; you'll see those two arrows adjacent to transistors, silicon controlled rectifiers, diodes— and they always mean the same thing when they are pointed

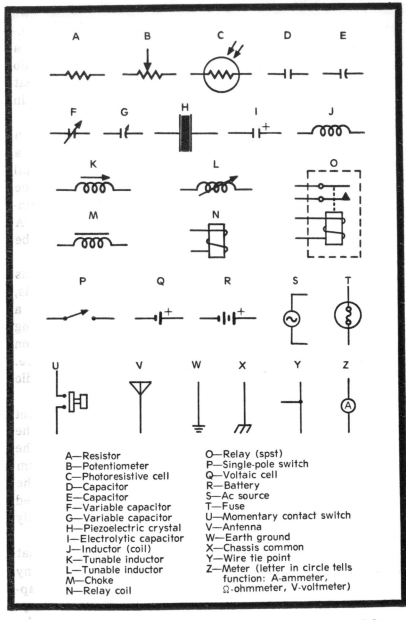

A—Resistor
B—Potentiometer
C—Photoresistive cell
D—Capacitor
E—Capacitor
F—Variable capacitor
G—Variable capacitor
H—Piezoelectric crystal
I—Electrolytic capacitor
J—Inductor (coil)
K—Tunable inductor
L—Tunable inductor
M—Choke
N—Relay coil

O—Relay (spst)
P—Single-pole switch
Q—Voltaic cell
R—Battery
S—Ac source
T—Fuse
U—Momentary contact switch
V—Antenna
W—Earth ground
X—Chassis common
Y—Wire tie point
Z—Meter (letter in circle tells
   function: A-ammeter,
   Ω-ohmmeter, V-voltmeter)

Fig. 4-4. Popular schematic symbols. How many do you recognize? Cover the lower portion of the page and try to name as many as you can. If you can't name more than 15, you'd better study the explanatory chart. You must be able to read schematic diagrams if you plan to build projects in other books.

toward the symbol. The resistive-cell drawing without the two arrows signifies a thermistor—a resistor that changes conductivity with temperature. Some thermistors exhibit a marked decrease in resistance when they get hot; others do just the opposite. Thermistors are used as fire and heat alarms, temperature control, and for voltage control in vacuum-tube circuits, to mention only a few applications.

Items F and G are simply two methods of depicting a variable capacitor. You learned earlier in the book that a capacitor consists of nothing more than a couple of metal plates separated by an insulator, or dielectric. The distance between the two plates, or the dielectric strength of the insulating material, determines the value of the capacitor. A variable capacitor allows the distance between the plates to be varied manually, normally between two specified values.

Item H is a piezoelectric element, normally referred to as a "crystal." Depending on its thickness, size, grain of its axis, a crystal can produce a tiny alternating voltage when a pressure is applied to it. Similarly, when a minute alternating voltage is applied, it vibrates physically. The rate of vibration is directly proportional to the variations in applied pressure. The crystal element as shown in the symbol is used in radio circuits because the output is very precise and stable.

Though the symbol for a crystal microphone is different from the one pictured in Fig. 4-4H, the operation is exactly the same: A diaphragm is mechanically attached to the piezoelectric element. When someone speaks, the diaphragm vibrates, thereby applying stress to the crystal element. The crystal supplies an alternating voltage analog of the applied pressure, which is subsequently fed to an amplifier and finally to a speaker.

The symbols shown in J, K, L, and M are all similar in that they are coils. Item J is a simple coil that could be of any length and be used in any one of a large variety of applications. A coil can be considered roughly to have the opposite function of capacitors; that is, while a capacitor blocks dc and passes ac, the coil blocks ac and passes dc. Much depends on the value of the coil, however. The capacitor is inherently a high-pass filter, allowing all frequencies over a specific value to pass while blocking all frequencies under that value. The coil is essentially a low-pass filter; depending on the value (expressed in henrys, millihenrys, or microhenrys), all frequencies under a specific value are allowed to pass, but all frequencies above that value are blocked. Coils and capacitors are frequently used together to block and pass in such a way that very stable one-frequency signals can be generated.

Items K and L are one and the same; they define a coil whose inductance may be varied by some means. Usually, the inductance of a coil is varied by means of a ferrite core that is screwed into and out of the coil's center. There are several methods of varying the inductance of a coil, but there is little standardization on the use of symbols to depict by which method the coil referenced is varied.

Item M is a coil, too. But the line above the coil (sometimes two lines are used) tells you the coil has a husky iron core. Coils of this type often resemble transformers, and they are called "chokes." A choke is used in series with a varying dc source to smooth the ripple content, turning the dc into a purer, more stable voltage source than it would otherwise be.

Item N, like M, is another coil. This one is the heart of a relay or solenoid. The core piece is used as an electromagnet, which performs some mechanical function. The symbol next to it (O) is the relay.

The symbols of Q and R are very similar. Item R, of course, is a battery. But a battery consists of more than one individual cell. The cell itself is represented by the symbol shown in Q. Notice the marked resemblance between the single cell and the capacitor, as depicted in schematic diagrams. The electrolytic capacitor consists of two parallel lines of equal length, however, while the cell consists of parallel lines of different lengths. The longer of the two parallel lines is always the positive terminal of the cell. Similarly, the battery symbol contains parallel lines of two lengths. The end with the longer line is always positive. If the line on each end of the battery is of the same length, the symbol has been incorrectly drawn.

There are some similarities between the symbols of S and T, but the similarity stops with the artwork. The horizontal S in the circle always represents an ac voltage source; it may mean a household outlet or it might mean an ac generator. Sometimes it is used to depict a sine-wave signal generator. The only thing you know for sure when you see this symbol is that an ac voltage is generated in the place where the circle is used. The other symbol, an S that is connected to the schematic diagram's power lines, depicts a fuse. It could bo used in ac or dc circuits, and might be any value, from a few milliamperes to thousands of amperes; usually, the value is printed adjacent to the symbol.

The triangle shown in V is an antenna. The fact that it is shown as a triangle does not mean that a specific con-figuration of antenna must be used. As a matter of fact, more often then not an ordinary piece of wire (very long, of course) will suffice, particularly in receiver circuits. If there is some particular requirement with regard to the type of antenna, its construction, etc., there will be a note on the diagram so stipulating.

The symbols of W and X have caused more furore in the electronics industry than any of the others—perhaps even more than all of the others put together. There is nothing complicated in them, I hasten to add; it's just that W was at one time used to denote what X depicts today. And instead of eliminating the symbol of W entirely, it was reassigned to depict another related function. The three horizontal parallel lines of diminshing size refer today to an earth ground. If you see this symbol on a modern schematic diagram, you will know that it means you are to connect the wire to a waterpipe, conduit, or other conductor that is physically sunk into the earth outside your home. In other words, it means "ground" in the most literal sense of the word.

The other symbol (X) is used to mean "ground" also; but when this symbol is shown, you need not make certain there is an actual earth-ground connection. You can use one heavy bus wire in whatever circuit you're building, and tie all "grounds" to this common line. If you're working with metal chassis, the chassis itself will undoubtedly be used as the common tie point. It is always good engineering practice, of course, to electrically ground all chassis to the earth anyway, so the differences between the two symbols aren't monumental; nonetheless, the "rake" ground, as it is called, simply means: "Tie all points marked this way to one common bus wire."

The final symbol in Fig. 4-4 is a meter. The letter in the circle will tell you the kind of meter you should use, and it might be anything from a simple voltmeter or ammeter to a complicated instrument such as an impedance-measuring meter.

There are other symbols for passive components, but these (and the transformer, of course) are the most common. As you work more and more in electronics, you'll get more and more familiar with the symbols in current use. If you learn the ones shown in this subsection and the active ones shown in the next, you're not likely to be "snowed" by any circuit that employs discrete (non-IC) components.

SEMICONDUCTOR DEVICES

It would be possible to include a large section on vacuum tubes, but these devices are being replaced more and more with transistors of one type or another, and the field of vacuum-tube devices gets more restrictive by the day. Instead, we concentrate on the more popular of the many available semiconductors. In Fig. 4-5, 22 schematic symbols are shown; some of these symbols are redundant—the tunnel diode, for example, may be depicted by either one of two schematic drawings. Look at the symbols before reading further; see how many you can recognize without looking at the explanatory text that accompanies the drawings. Try to familiarize yourself with the basic diode sketches, and see how an additional mark or line can change the meaning of the symbol.

Bipolar Transistors

Sketches A, M, N, T, and U are all representative of bipolar transistors, but what are the differences between

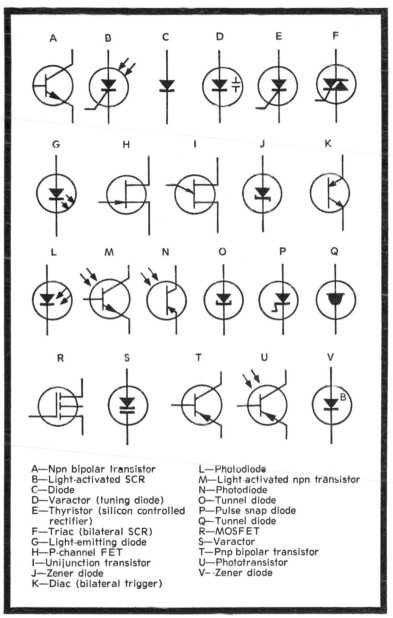

A—Npn bipolar transistor
B—Light-activated SCR
C—Diode
D—Varactor (tuning diode)
E—Thyristor (silicon controlled rectifier)
F—Triac (bilateral SCR)
G—Light-emitting diode
H—P-channel FET
I—Unijunction transistor
J—Zener diode
K—Diac (bilateral trigger)

L—Photodiode
M—Light-activated npn transistor
N—Photodiode
O—Tunnel diode
P—Pulse snap diode
Q—Tunnel diode
R—MOSFET
S—Varactor
T—Pnp bipolar transistor
U—Phototransistor
V—Zener diode

Fig. 4-5. The symbols on these two pages are but a few of the solid-state discrete components in current use in the electronics industry. How many can you recognize? Cover the answers and try to name them. Devices D and S are the same, like two ways of spelling a word; similarly, devices J and V are identical, as are L and N and O and Q.

them? Items A and T should be relatively easy; you've been working with these in projects presented earlier in this book. A is an npn transistor, and T is a pnp equivalent. The arrow direction on the emitter tells you whether the bipolar transistor in pnp or npn. In npn devices, the arrow points away from the transistor junction; in pnp devices, the arrow contacts the junction. Both M and U are phototransistors; M is an npn, and U is a pnp type. The symbol shown in sketch N is often used to depict a photodiode, but it really refers to a phototransistor that has no base lead.

An interesting fact is that **all** bipolar transistors are photoelectric devices! One of the peculiar characteristics of the transistor junction is the fact that current will flow in the emitter-collector circuit when light strikes it. The phenomenon isn't observable most of the time, of course, because transistors are packaged in light-tight cases, either black plastic or metal. To make a phototransistor, the manufacturer places an ordinary bipolar transistor in a case designed to allow as much light as possible to fall on the surface of the junction. This typically means housing the device in a clean epoxy case, but in many phototransistors a collimating lens is built into the case to concentrate large quantities of light onto the junction.

Diodes

Knowing that a pair of arrows adjacent to a schematic symbol identifies the device as a light-operating type, you should have little trouble recognizing some of the diode symbols. Members of the diode family are those symbols pictured in sketches B, C, D, E, F, G, J, L, O, P, Q, S, and V.

The simplest of the diode devices is pictured in C; it is a simple rectifier diode that allows current to pass through it in one direction only. Electron flow begins at the cathode (the short line perpendicular to the connecting lines) and goes through the diode in a direction opposite to the arrow. Since **conventional current flow** is considered to go from plus to minus, however, rather than minus to plus, the arrow was incorporated into the drawing as shown. You can think of current flowing in the direction of the arrow if you like, as long as you remember that **conventional current flow** is opposite the actual flow of electrons.

Sketch D is one way of showing the deivce depicted by S—a varactor, or tuning diode. In this device, the junction between the positive and negative impurities is separated by an undoped region of the intrinsic semiconductor material, which serves as a dielectric, or nonconductor. In many ways, the diode acts as a conventional capacitor. However, because of the "negatlve-resistance" characteristic of the junction under certain applied-voltage conditions, the value of capacitance can be changed in direct proportion to the applied bias voltage. The varactor has many uses because of the negative-resistance characteristic, but the most common is simply as a substitute for a manually variable capacitor.

Sketches B and E are very similar, with one exception: B is light-operated while E is not. Both are thyristors, often called "silicon controlled rcctifiers" or four-layer diodes. The basic thyristor, shown in sketch E, is a thyristor of npnp construction. The three terminals are the **anode**, the **cathode**, and the **gate**. The cathode is the short line perpendicular to the connecting line, as it is in the ordinary diode. The anode Is shown at the top. The gate element, which triggers the device into conduction, is the line from the sidc that connects at the symbol's junction. The thyristor is used in dc switching circuits to serve in much the same manner as a relay. Thyristors can handle fairly large amounts of power from cathode to anode, so the device is inserted in a high-current is allowed to flow, the thyristor remains an open switch. As soon as a small gate current is introduced, however, the anode-cathode "switch" closes, and current flows in the circuit being controlled.

Sketch B operates the same way, except that gate current flows automatically as soon as light strikes the surface of the device's lens. An interesting characteristic of thyristors of both types is that once the anode-cathode circuit closes, it stays closed—even when the gate current is removed entirely. This phenomenon has both good points and bad. A ood point is that the electronic switch can be made to trigger with no more than a quick pulse, which makes it kin to the latching relay. A disadvantage, though, is that some means for shutting down the switch must be incorporated in the circuit design. In burglar alarms and similar applications, the thyristor can be shut off by the mere expedient of manually opening the anode-cathode circuit momentarily. In remote-control applications, thyristor shutoff can be problemsome and complex.

The strange-looking symbol shown in sketch F is officially referred to as a "bilateral thyristor," or, more popularly, a "triac." Operationally, the triac is the same as a pair of thyristors cross-connected, and with a single gate. In practice, the triac allows switching of dc or ac on a nonlatching basis. You can consider the triac, for all practical purposes, as an ac relay. There is no cathode or anode, since the upper and lower terminals are the same: so these terminals are simply numbered 1 and 2. The gate is referenced to terminal 1, and when gate current is caused to flow, the two main terminals "close," allowing high-current loads to be controlled. Since the triac can be made to trigger with lightning-fast speeds, the device is used in lamp dimmers and motor speed control applications by turning on and off the household power at a specified rate.

The symbol shown in sketch G has the two arrows that mark it as a light-operated device, but notice that the arrows point outward rather than inward toward the device's junction. Outward arrows mean the unit actually generates light. This symbol, then, represents the light-emitting diode. When proper dc bias is applied, the light-emitting diode glows a bright red (or green, depending on the structure of the junction). The unit is used extensively in indicators, readouts, and other such applications because it generates a lot of light and very little heat, making it one of our most efficient light sources. Also, since it is of solid-state construction, it has a virtually unlimited lifetime.

Sketches J and V are the same—different ways of showing the zener diode. (The B in the circle of sketch V refers to "breakdown," because it is the zener's breakdown point that determines its value.) The zener is a natural voltage regulator. Beneath the breakdown voltage point, the zener seems much the same as any other simple diode. When sufficient voltage is applied to reach the device's breakdown point, however, the diode will conduct in a reverse direction. Almost without regard to the amount of applied voltage, the voltage drop across the zener will remain the same as the voltage it saw at breakdown. A 12V zener will maintain a cathode-to-anode potential of 12V when more than 12V is applied, and the voltage across it remains 12V no matter how high the input voltage goes. Since the zener must dissipate the excess voltage (over and above the breakdown point), it must be capable of handling the power excesses; otherwise, the heat of the dissipated power will destroy the semiconductor.

Sketch L is a photodiode; it conducts as long as light strikes the surface of the junction. When the light is removed, the diode ceases to conduct. Sometimes the symbol is used interchangeably with the baseless transistor diagram of sketch N.

Sketches O and Q are two ways of depicting a tunnel diode, a varactor-like device that has a negative-resistance characteristic and can switch fast enough from one state to another to make it ideal for very high frequency and microwave oscillator applications. The pulse magnitude is so high on the output of these devices that they can actually be used as amplifiers.

The pulse snap diode is shown in sketch P. You won't be using these, probably, because they aren't typically found in hobby circuits. They are used where ultrafast switching is required. Typical applications include pulse generation, waveshaping, and the like.

Unipolar Transistors

A unipolar transistor is a transistor that has but one junction. Both field-effect and unijunction transistors fit this category.

The junction-type field-effect transistor is shown in sketch H. If you've been building some of the projects shown in this book, you've probably already had the chance to work with it. Since we discussed the device at some length in the section including the projects, we won't go into the technical aspects here. The important point is for you to note the difference between the junction FET and the insulated-gate FET shown in sketch R.

In the insulated-gate FET, there is no direct connection between the gate and the junction. A thin coating of oxide separates the gate capacitively from the junction, which serves to increase the device's input impedance considerably. The insulation is so thin and fragile that even a touch at the gate of an unprotected device can cause a static-electricity discharge that can destroy the device. If you work with insulated-gate FETs (also called MOSFETs), you must take certain precautionary measures to avoid damaging the FET before you even have applied power to the circuit you've built!

You've used the unijunction (sketch I) and presumably have read some of the technical aspects of the device, so we can go on to the bilateral trigger, or "trigger diode," shown in sketch K.

The trigger diode, popularly referred to as a "diac," is typically used in conjunction with a triac to control ac loads. The diac is characterized by the need for a specific firing voltage, which must be applied to the unit before triggering can take place.

Now you've made at least a passing acquaintance with the more common members of the growing family of semiconductors. Study the sketches and learn the basics of them, then go to work on the remaining circuits in this book. You're on your own from here on; you must do all the layout, design, parts listing. All we're giving you are the circuits.

Project 14

Low-Voltage DC Power Supply

If you skipped over the power supply circuit of Fig. 4-2, you're missing out on a real potential money-saver. The circuit is that of a full-wave bridge-type power supply. It plugs into a household outlet and converts the 115V ac power to the 9V dc level required by most of the circuit projects shown in this book.

The power supply has other things going for it, too. It is simple enough to use a first-project layout try. The number of parts is small enough that you should be able to determine the size requirements before beginning construction, then buy the parts and reduce the design to actual "hardware" in a matter of an hour or less. Projects such as this will give you the confidence you need to tackle the bigger or more complex circuits.

There is nothing critical about the diodes, so no part numbers were given. When you go to the neighborhood electronics dealer, simply order four diodes that will handle up to an ampere of current with a peak-inverse-voltage rating of 25V or so.

Since the output voltage of the circuit is to be about 9V dc, an electrolytic capacitor with a working voltage of 15V dc will be more than adequate.

There is a fuse in the circuit. You can eliminate this, of course; but it is good engineering practice to include a fuse in every power supply project, regardless of the output power of the supply. Fuses come in a wide variety of sizes and shapes, so take your pick. The rating should be 0.1A.

Does it seem strange that the fuse is rated at 0.1A when the output may be as high as 1A? There is no mistake; the fuse is in the transformer's primary circuit, where current is very low and voltage high. In the secondary, the voltage is reduced but the current is increased. The power in the primary circuit is substantially the same as the power in the secondary.

If you use a 0.1A fuse in the primary of the transformer, it means that you are allowing the transformer to draw no more than about 11.5W from the household power line. If the transformer is suddenly required to deliver more power than this, the fuse will blow. Volts multiplied by amperes equal total power. You are allowing the secondary to deliver as much as 10V (actually a bit less) at a current of 1A. If the load current increases much beyond this, the diodes will be destroyed. Since 10V multiplied by 1A is equal to 10W, you insert a fuse in the primary that will blow when the transformer draws more than this amount. The transformer's primary circuit operates on 115V approximately; so a fuse of 0.1A will limit the input power to 0.1 times 115, or 11.5W.

Project 15

Sound-Activated Relay

If you build the circuit of Fig. 4-6, you'll get the chance to use quite a number of the devices you've met in this section. The circuit is a sound-activated relay that allows you to control almost any circuit with a word or clap of the hand.

In many ways, the circuit resembles the touch switch presented in an earlier section: A field-effect transistor drives an npn bipolar transistor that is used to control the pnp relay driver. The relay itself, however, is controlled by a silicon controlled rectifier, or thyristor. The thyristor is used because of its latching characteristic; once it has been triggered, it holds the relay in the on state until the momentary-contact switch interrupts the anode-cathode circuit in the thyristor.

The relay in the circuit can be eliminated entirely if the load to be controlled (1) is operated from the same voltage used to operate the circuit, (2) requires no more current than the thyristor is capable of handling, and (3) the dc resistance of the load is less than a couple of thousand ohms.

When you plan your layout, be sure to allow space for the potentiometer, the relay, and the microphone. Remember, too, that electrolytic capacitors are sized according to their value; high-value electrolytics are larger than low-value units.

In operation, the sensitivity of the device is controlled by the 5K potentiometer (linear taper) in the drain circuit of the high-impedance junction FET. Since the momentary-contact switch is used to reset the circuit after it has been triggered, you must also remember that this switch is a normally closed type rather than the normally open switch that you have used in earlier circuit projects.

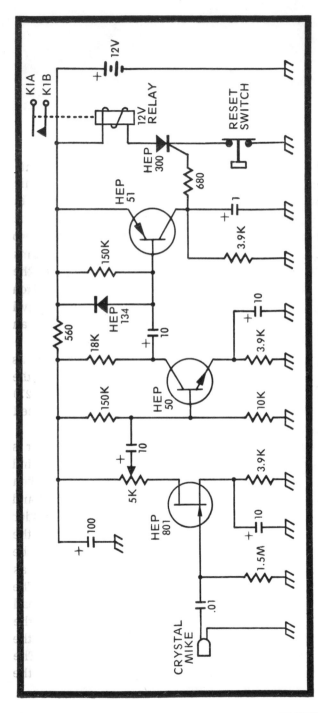

Fig. 4-6. Noise-activated switch schematic. You may use the contacts of the relay (K1A and K1B) to control any load, ac or dc, as long as the load current does not exceed the rating of the contacts. For miniature burglar-alarm applications, where a low-current buzzer or the equivalent is employed, you can connect the buzzer in place of the relay coil. Read the text, though, to make certain the load fulfills the criteria necessitated by the HEP 300 thyristor. (Circuit courtesy Motorola.)

Project 16

Transistor Siren

The siren circuit shown in Fig. 4-7 is a little electronic assembly that Motorola engineers like to refer to as a "panic button." The unit incorporates two switches; the one shown in the battery circuit is the power switch, the other is a momentary-contact type (normally open) that is used to trigger the siren. When you press the button, the siren begins its long, slow upward wail. When you release the button, the wail starts downward. The wail is extremely "lifelike," which makes this circuit ideal for such applications as boating, civil defense, etc. Of course, when it is used for serious purposes, an amplifier must be used with it.

To incorporate an amplifier right on the same chassis as the siren itself, simply substitute a fixed resistor for the speaker (the resistor can be any value between 120 and 270 ohms), then take the signal from across the resistor to feed into the amplifier.

The coil in the collector circuit of the first pnp transistor is simple to make from enameled wire. All you have to do is wind 550 turns of 30 gage wire around a ten-penny nail. When you get to the halfway point in your winding (275 turns), stop and scrape a small section of the enamel off the wire, and solder the end of another piece to the scraped area. The length of the soldered-on piece is not critical—five or six inches should be sufficient. Make the solder connection as neat (not bulky) as you can, then finish winding the wire around the nail. The short piece of wire you soldered on the coil connects to the lead joining the two switches. The inside end of the coil goes to the capacitor feeding the base of the first pnp transistor; the outside end goes to the collector of the same transistor. The coil is used to feed part of the transistor's signal back to the input in a proper phase relation to the input.

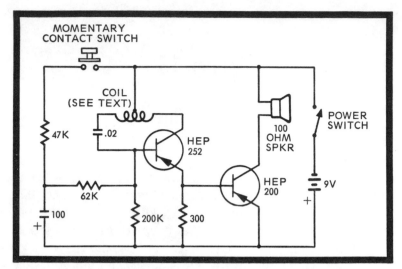

Fig. 4-7. Two-transistor electronic siren. The capacitors are all 15V types; resistors are quarter-watt units. This unit will easily fit on a 3 x 4 phenolic board, even with the speaker and battery. If you use a plastic box to contain the assembly, mount both switches on the outside of the box. Melt a number of small holes to serve as a speaker grille.

The speaker can be anything from 60 to 100 ohms. Motorola recommends a Quam 22A06A 100, which is a 100-ohm miniature speaker that will fit nicely into a standard plastic box of the type used on previous projects.

Project 17
Model Railroad Wigwag

Whether your model railroad is HO or N gage, you're sure to find a place for a realistic set of railroad blinkers. The circuit shown in Fig. 4-8 is the electronics portion; the mechanical part is up to you.

The red flashing blinkers are a couple of Motorola light-emitting diodes (HEP P2003). The switching circuit is a simple multivibrator made up of a couple of pnp transistors (HEP S0006). A timing circuit of resistors and capacitors establishes the duration of each blink as well as the period between flashes.

The light-emitting diodes used in this circuit are ideal for model railroad applications because they are tiny, dome-shaped, very bright when illuminated, and red. You should have no trouble incorporating the assembly in the base of a commercially available wigwag model.

If the wigwag model is plastic, you can mount the LEDs in the wigwag arms by melting small holes in which to seat the diodes. A couple of very fine wire pairs (32-gage, for example), from the base-mounted electronics to the light-emitting diodes, should be fairly easy to hide.

If you have the chance, examine the hobby components before you buy. You might even be able to get a unit with a hollow shaft; this would be ideal for carrying the wires.

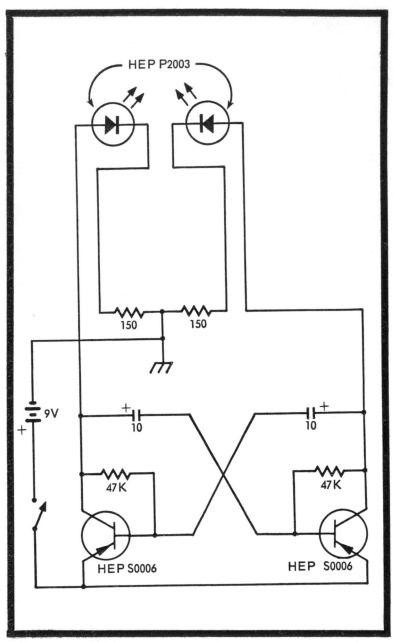

Fig. 4-8. This blinker circuit is ideal for model railroad applications. When the switch is closed, the two bright LEDs flash alternately. The switch can be eliminated if your railroad has an automatic triggering mechanism.

Project 18

Automatic Rooster

If you like to wake up with the chickens but find no barn-yards in your neighborhood, you might try building our "automatic rooster," shown in Fig. 4-9. It's actually an electronic alarm that is triggered by the breaking dawn.

Your house probably has a wealth of alarm clocks, which you can set to go off whenever you like. But if you like camping out on hunting trips, this little device will roust you out before you sleep through a few possible kills.

It has more practical applications, too. As a burglar alarm, the unit can be placed anywhere there isn't supposed to be light. The light sensitivity is great enough that even flickering flames will trigger it, so you can use it as a fire alarm, too.

The circuit consists of a photodiode, an npn transistor, a couple of small capacitors, a resistor, a tiny audio trans-former, and a miniature speaker. The npn transistor is connected in an oscillator configuration so that when light strikes the photodiode, a portion of the npn's signal is fed back to the input in phase with the input signal. The feedback signal flows through the emitter-collector circuit of the photodiode when the photodiode is illuminated. Removing the light breaks the circuit and there is no feedback (thus, no signal).

The transformer provides the necessary phase inversion to counter the natural phase inversion of the npn transistor. The npn's base sees a coupled signal that is 360 degrees out of phase with its regular input—another way of saying the signal is exactly in phase.

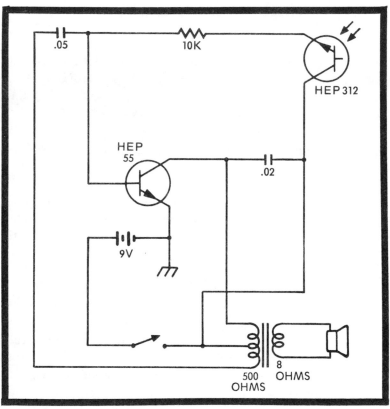

Fig. 4-9. This "electronic rooster" is actually a light-activated alarm. As soon as light strikes the junction of the HEP 312 photodiode, a loud oscillator signal can be heard from the speaker. (Circcuit courtesy Motorola.)

Project 19

Burglar Alarm Trigger

If you built the alarm warbler circuit described in Project 13, you might be looking for an effective means of triggering the alarm for "watchguard" applications. The circuit shown in Fig. 4-10 is particularly good as an alarm trigger because it is reliable, simple, and inexpensive.

An ordinary thyristor is used to activate a dc relay. The thyristor's stay-on characteristic is put to excellent use in this circuit; once triggered, the alarm can only be shut down by pressing a covertly placed reset switch.

A length of foil strip (you can substitute switches in place of the foil strip if you like) connects a 470-ohm resistor in the thyristor's gate circuit to ground. The resistor biases the gate at such a low voltage that no current is permitted to flow. If the resistor is lifted from ground, however—accomplished by interrupting the circuit by a break in the foil strip (or an opening of a switch in that line)—gate potential is increased considerably and current flows.

When gate current flows in the thyristor, the anode-cathode circuit closes, which energizes the relay. To shut the alarm off, the anode-cathode circuit must be broken.

The diode shunting the relay coil is a must if you want to protect the thyristor from inductive spikes that typically accompany the making and breaking of a dc circuit feeding a coil (transformer action).

If you connect this circuit to your car battery, you don't need to worry about current drain. Even though the circuit is operating as long as voltage is connected, the total current drain (before being triggered, that is) is only slightly more than 1 milliampere. You can calculate the current by using Ohm's law: current drain in amperes is equal to voltage

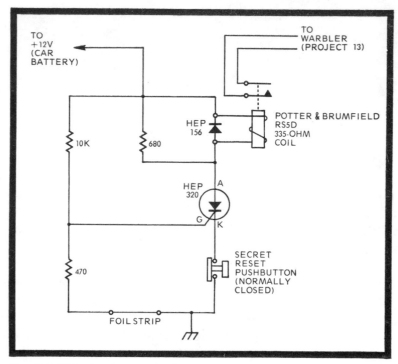

Fig. 4-10. This simple circuit, when used with an alarm device, can be an effective deterrent to theft. The foil strip can be replaced by a series of normally closed door switches. The idea is to set off the alarm if the 470-ohm resistor's ground path is interrupted. The K identifier on the thyristor is often used to identify the cathode.

divided by resistance. When the thyristor is open-circuited, the total circuit current is developed by the two series resistances, the 10K and the 470-ohm resistor. This total resistance (10,470 ohms), divided into 12.000V, equals about 0.0015A, or 1.5 mA.

Project 20
Novelty Fuse Tester

As the last project in this book, we're including a circuit you can really have some fun with. Without a fuse in the circuit, and a 9V battery installed properly, the two pilot lamps will flash continuously.

It may be that there aren't too many practical applications for flashing lamps. Bob Brown, who contributed the circuit, could think of but one—a very deluxe battery tester. If you plug a battery into the circuit and the lamps flash, you know the battery is capable of generating a little power.

The fuseholder is an ingenious touch, however, if you have a pocket full of holders you don't plan using for something important. When you press the pushbutton when a fuse is in the holder, the fuse blows. When the fuse blows, the voltage to the flasher circuit is interrupted, so the lamps stop working.

When you hand the completed assembly to someone (along with a fuse for him to test, of course) you're taking advantage of a very basic human frailty: the almost uncontrollable urge to push buttons. Place a sign on the box that says, **IF LAMPS FLASH, FUSE IS GOOD.** When the unsuspecting button pusher inserts the fuse, the lamps will flash, indicating that the fuse is indeed in good working order. But if your "patsy" is anything at all like his fellow men, he won't be satisfied at that. He'll press the convenient pushbutton. The lamps will stop flashing. And you'll have to come up with another fuse. So who's the REAL patsy?

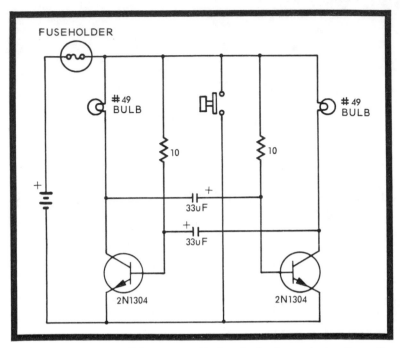

Fig. 4-11. You can use this as a novelty fuse tester by enclosing the entire circuit in a plastic box. In plain letters, write: IF LAMPS FLASH, FUSE IS GOOD. The urge to press buttons is too much for most people; and when they press the button the fuse goes.

INDEX